Simulating Water Temperature of the Klamath River under Dam Removal and Climate Change Scenarios

By Russell W. Perry, John C. Risley, Scott J. Brewer, Edward C. Jones, and Dennis W. Rondorf

Open-File Report 2011-1243

U.S. Department of the Interior
U.S. Geological Survey

U.S. Department of the Interior
KEN SALAZAR, Secretary

U.S. Geological Survey
Marcia K. McNutt, Director

U.S. Geological Survey, Reston, Virginia: 2011

For more information on the USGS—the Federal source for science about the Earth,
its natural and living resources, natural hazards, and the environment,
visit http://www.usgs.gov or call 1–888–ASK–USGS.

For an overview of USGS information products, including maps, imagery, and publications,
visit http://www.usgs.gov/pubprod

To order this and other USGS information products, visit http://store.usgs.gov

Suggested citation:
Perry, R.W., Risley, J.C., Brewer, S.J., Jones, E.C., and Rondorf, D.W., 2011, Simulating daily water temperatures of
the Klamath River under dam removal and climate change scenarios: U.S. Geological Survey Open-File Report 2011-
1243, 78 p.

Contents

Figures

Tables

Conversion Factors and Datums

Multiply	By	To obtain
Length		
foot (ft)	0.3048	meter (m)
mile (mi)	1.609	kilometer (km)
Area		
Acre	4,047	square meter (m^2)
Acre	0.004047	square kilometer (km^2)
square foot (ft^2)	0.09290	square meter (m^2)
square mile (mi^2)	2.590	square kilometer (km^2)
Volume		
cubic foot (ft^3)	0.02832	cubic meter (m^3)
Flow rate		
acre-foot per day (acre-ft/d)	0.01427	cubic meter per second (m^3/s)
cubic foot per second (ft^3/s)	0.02832	cubic meter per second (m^3/s)
Pressure		
milibar (mb)	0.1	kilopascal (kPa)
Energy		
Langley per day (Ly/day)	0.0001167	kilocalories per meter squared per second (kcal/m^2/s)

Temperature in degrees Celsius (°C) may be converted to degrees Fahrenheit (°F) as follows:
°F=(1.8×°C)+32.
Temperature in degrees Fahrenheit (°F) may be converted to degrees Celsius (°C) as follows:
°C=(°F-32)/1.8.

Datums

Coordinate information is referenced to North American Datum of 1983 (NAD 83).
Altitude, as used in this report, refers to distance above the vertical datum.

Abbreviations and Acronyms

AME	Absolute mean error
BO	Biological Opinion
BOR	Bureau of Reclamation
CCCMA	Canadian Centre for Climate Modeling Analysis
GCM	Global Circulation Models
GFDL	Geophysical Fluid Dynamics Laboratory
KBRA	Klamath Basin Restoration Agreement
KHSA	Klamath Hydroelectric Settlement Agreement
ME	Mean error
MIUB	Meteorological Research Institute of the University of Bonn
MRI	Meteorological Research Institute
NMFS	National Marine Fisheries Service
NSCE	Nash-Sutcliffe statistic
RBM10	River Basin Model-10
RM	River Mile
RMSE	Root mean square error
TMDL	Total Maximum Daily Load
USBR	U.S. Bureau of Reclamation
USFS	U.S. Forest Service
USFWS	U.S. Fish and Wildlife Service
USGS NWIS	U.S. Geological Survey National Water Information System
USGS FORT	U.S. Geological Survey Fort Collins Science Center.
WY	Water year

Simulating Water Temperature of the Klamath River under Dam Removal and Climate Change Scenarios

By Russell W. Perry, John C. Risley, Scott J. Brewer, Edward C. Jones, and Dennis W. Rondorf

Abstract

A one-dimensional daily averaged water temperature model was used to simulate Klamath River temperatures for two management alternatives under historical climate conditions and six future climate scenarios. The analysis was conducted for the Secretarial Determination on removal of four hydroelectric dams on the Klamath River. In 2012, the Secretary of the Interior will determine if dam removal and implementation of the Klamath Basin Restoration Agreement (KBRA) (Klamath Basin Restoration Agreement, 2010) will advance restoration of salmonid fisheries and is in the public interest. If the Secretary decides dam removal is appropriate, then the four dams are scheduled for removal in 2020.

Water temperature simulations were conducted to compare the effect of two management alternatives: the no-action alternative where dams remain in place, and the action alternative where dam removal occurs in 2020 along with habitat restoration. Each management alternative was simulated under historical climate conditions (1961–2010) and six 50-year (2012–2061) climate scenarios. The model selected for the study, River Basin Model-10 (RBM10), was used to simulate water temperatures over a 253-mile reach of the Klamath River located in south-central Oregon and northern California. RBM10 uses a simple equilibrium flow model, assuming discharge in each river segment on each day is transmitted downstream instantaneously. The model uses a heat budget formulation to quantify heat flux at the air-water interface. Inputs for the heat budget were calculated from daily-mean meteorological data, including net shortwave solar radiation, net longwave atmospheric radiation, air temperature, wind speed, vapor pressure, and a psychrometric constant needed to calculate the Bowen ratio. The modeling domain was divided into nine reaches ranging in length from 10.8 to 42.4 miles, which were calibrated and validated separately with measured water temperature data collected irregularly from 1961 to 2010. Calibration root mean square errors of observed versus simulated water temperatures for the nine reaches ranged from 0.8 to 1.5°C. Mean absolute errors ranged from 0.6 to 1.2°C. For model validation, a k-fold cross-validation technique was used. Validation root mean square error and mean absolute error for the nine reaches ranged from 0.8 to 1.4°C and 0.8 to 1.2°C, respectively.

Input data for the six future climate scenarios (2012–2061) were derived from historical hydrological and meteorological data and simulated meteorological output from five Global Circulation Models. Total Maximum Daily Loads or other regulatory processes that might reduce future water temperatures were not included in the simulations. Under the current climate conditions scenario, impacts of dam removal on water temperatures were greatest near Iron Gate Dam (near Yreka, California) and were attenuated in the lower reaches of the Klamath River. May and October simulated mean water temperatures increased and decreased by approximately 1–2°C and 2–4°C, respectively, downstream of Iron Gate Dam after dam removal. Dam removal also resulted in an earlier annual temperature cycle shift of 18 days, 5 days, and 2 days, near Iron Gate Dam, Scott River, and Trinity River, respectively. Although the magnitude of precipitation and air temperature change predicted by the five Global Circulation Models varied, all five models resulted in progressive incremental increases in water temperatures with each decade from 2012 to 2061. However, dam removal under KBRA appeared to delay the effects of climate change to some extent near Iron Gate Dam. With dam removal under KBRA, annual-mean water temperatures exceeded the 49-year historical mean temperature beginning in 2045; whereas with dams, annual-mean temperatures exceeded the historical mean beginning in 2025.

Potential changes in seasonal water temperatures resulting from dam removal, with or without future climate change, have a direct impact on fisheries in the Klamath Basin. Water temperature changes are of particular interest in spring (April–May) when salmon smolts out-migrate to the Pacific Ocean, and in fall (October–November) when Chinook salmon return upstream to spawn.

Introduction

Background

The Klamath Basin has seen considerable controversy over water-related resource issues in the past century as agriculture, forestry, hydropower, and fish and wildlife interests have competed for scarce water resources. In 2010, the Klamath Basin stakeholders came together to sign the Klamath Hydroelectric Settlement Agreement (KHSA) (Klamath Hydroelectric Settlement Agreement, 2010) and the KBRA. In the agreements, the Basin's stakeholders agreed to move toward removal of the lower four hydroelectric dams (J.C. Boyle, Copco 1, Copco 2, and Iron Gate) on the Klamath River owned by PacifiCorp, with removal of the dams scheduled for 2020.

As a result of the KBRA and KHSA agreements, the Secretary of Interior, in cooperation with the Secretary of Commerce and other federal agencies, was tasked with making a decision on alternative management actions for a 50-year period of interest (2012–2061). The review, evaluation, and decision are hereafter referred to as the Secretarial Determination. The two management alternatives being reviewed for the Secretarial Determination and in this report are:

No Action Alternative: Assumes no change from the current management, which includes on-going programs under existing laws and authorities that contribute to the continued existence of listed threatened and endangered species and Tribal Trust species (Hamilton and others, 2010).

Action Alternative: Removal of the lower four Klamath River dams (J.C. Boyle, Copco 1, Copco 2, and Iron Gate) in the year 2020, and implementation of the actions and restoration programs in KBRA. This is the action alternative that would be pursued if a positive finding is made in the Secretarial Determination.

The Secretary will make a determination by March 31, 2012. The criteria for the decision are (1) will the proposed action advance restoration of the salmonid fisheries of the Klamath Basin, and (2) is the action in the public interest, which includes, but is not limited to, consideration of potential impacts on affected local communities and Tribes.

Salmon populations are influenced by a myriad of habitat and environmental conditions, including water temperatures in habitats ranging from natal streams to the Pacific Ocean. Salmon in the Klamath River are near the southern limit of the range for salmonids, so water temperature is an important environmental variable. Water temperature is important to all aspects of the life history of salmonids including growth, incubation, sexual maturation, and as a cue for the onset of juvenile and adult migration behavior. Temperature also is an important determinant of the host-pathogen relations for salmon and can play a role in prespawning mortality. Water temperature also is a key water-quality parameter because of its central role in determining rates of nutrient cycling and productivity of aquatic ecosystems in the phosphorus-rich Klamath Basin waters.

The evaluation for the Secretarial Determination includes water temperatures under the no action (dams in place) and action alternatives (dams removed with KBRA implementation). Dam removal proposed under KBRA is partially aimed at modifying water temperature to make conditions more desirable for salmonids. Dams, reservoirs, and the associated modifications to the hydrologic regime can alter thermal regimes and thereby affect salmonids. The surface area and hydraulic residence time of reservoirs are key physical factors in the summer warming of reservoir waters compared to free-flowing riverine environments. Bartholow and others (2005) modeled water temperature of the Klamath River with and without dams. They found a phase shift of about 18 days in the thermal signature of dams compared to predicted conditions with dams removed. The predicted summer maxima and winter minima occurred about 18 days earlier without dams. Deas and Orlob (1999) modeled water quality and divided issues into two categories: water temperature and other water-quality parameters (for example, dissolved oxygen, nutrients). They found increasing flow reduced the transit time in the study reach from Iron Gate Dam to Seiad Valley and moderated the diurnal temperature range providing modest temperature benefits.

Developments in recent years have led to additional water temperature modeling, which we present in this report. The U.S. Fish and Wildlife Service (USFWS) is currently preparing a new biological opinion (BO) for endangered suckers (U.S. Fish and Wildlife Service, 2008). The National Marine Fisheries Service (NMFS) issued a new biological opinion for coho salmon in 2010 (National Marine Fisheries Service, 2010). The guidance in the recent KBRA and KHSA agreements provide a new paradigm for flow management on the Klamath River. Recently, modeled flows and predicted changes in flows associated with climate change have been conducted for the Secretarial Determination (Greimann and others, 2011). These new sources of information on flows, management scenarios, and climate change made a compelling case for a renewed effort to model water temperature in the Klamath River for the Secretarial Determination. The River Basin Model-10 (RBM10) was reviewed and selected for use for this modeling effort (Yearsley and others, 2001; Yearsley, 2009).

The RBM10 model is well suited to the temporal, spatial, and structural requirements for simulating water temperatures in the Klamath Basin. We required a model that could (1) predict mean daily water temperature along a longitudinal gradient of a river, (2) accommodate both reservoir and river sections, and (3) quickly simulate long time series (50 years). In addition, RBM10 was used to develop Total Maximum Daily Load (TMDL) for temperature, simulate impounded and free-flowing conditions, and predict climate change effects on the Snake and Columbia Rivers (Yearsley, 2009). Our goals were quite similar for the Klamath River, making RBM10 an excellent candidate model for our needs. RMB10 is a 1-dimensional water temperature model and therefore assumes that water temperature in reservoir segments is vertically and laterally homogeneous. Although Iron Gate Reservoir stratifies during the summer, we felt that RBM10 may perform satisfactorily due to short water residence time in the reservoir.

Purpose and Scope

Our goal for this study was to assess the potential impacts of management scenarios and future changes in climate on water temperature. Daily water temperature of the Klamath River from Link River Dam (RM 253.0, RM = river mile) to the ocean was simulated for the two water management alternatives over a 50-year period using a range of climate scenarios. To provide a baseline against which to compare these simulations, we also reconstructed a 49-year record of historical water temperatures in the Klamath River. We first describe in detail how we built RBM10 for the Klamath River. Next, we conduct an extensive calibration and validation to observed historical water temperatures in the Klamath River. We then used the calibrated model to simulate water temperatures under the two water management alternatives and six climate scenarios, resulting in twelve 50-year simulations of water temperatures.

Study Site

The Klamath River originates in the Cascade Mountains of southern Oregon and flows through northern California to the Pacific Ocean. Its headwaters are fed by underground springs; the Williamson, Wood, and Sprague Rivers; and Lake Ewauna (fig. 1). Historically, water flowed from Upper Klamath Lake into Lower Klamath Lake by way of the Link River and Lake Ewauna before making its descent to the Pacific Ocean (Weddel, 2000). Lower Klamath Lake was drained in the early part of the 20th century and is now managed as a refuge for waterfowl and other wetland dependent species. Upper Klamath Lake is controlled by the Link River Dam. The modeled reach for this study begins at Link River Dam and continues 253 mi downstream to the Pacific Ocean.

The Klamath River basin covers more than 12,000 mi^2 and is divided into two subbasins (upper and lower) at Iron Gate Dam. The upper basin area includes parts of Klamath County in Oregon, and Siskiyou and Modoc Counties in California. The lower basin area includes parts of the Siskiyou, Modoc, Trinity, Humboldt, and Del Norte Counties in California. The Klamath River basin is unlike most watersheds with a unique geomorphology opposite of that found in most other drainage basins and has been called "a river upside down" by the National Geographic Society (Rymer, 2008). Much of the upper Oregon portion of the basin is flat and open, in comparison to the narrow canyons and mountainous terrain present in the lower California portion of the basin.

The upper Klamath River basin sits in the rainshadow of the Cascade Range on the west, the Deschutes River basin on the north, the Great Basin on the east, and the Pit River basin on the south. The upper basin consists of mostly agriculture and rangeland with areas of pine forest and semi-arid high desert plateaus, and is characterized by low relief, volcanic geology with an average annual precipitation of 34.89 in. (California Rivers Assessment, 2011). The lower Klamath River basin is mostly forested except for areas of agriculture and rangeland in the drainages of the Scott and Shasta Rivers. The basin is dominated by a steep, rugged, complex terrain, and alluvial reaches. Average annual precipitation for the lower basin is 79.62 in. (California Rivers Assessment, 2011).

For the purposes of the water temperature model, the study area is divided into nine model reaches designated along the Klamath River and indicated in figure 1. The reaches begin at the Link River Dam near Klamath Falls, Oregon (RM 253.1), with the first reach ending at RM 231.9 just downstream of Keno Dam, and the ninth and last reach ending at RM 5.7.

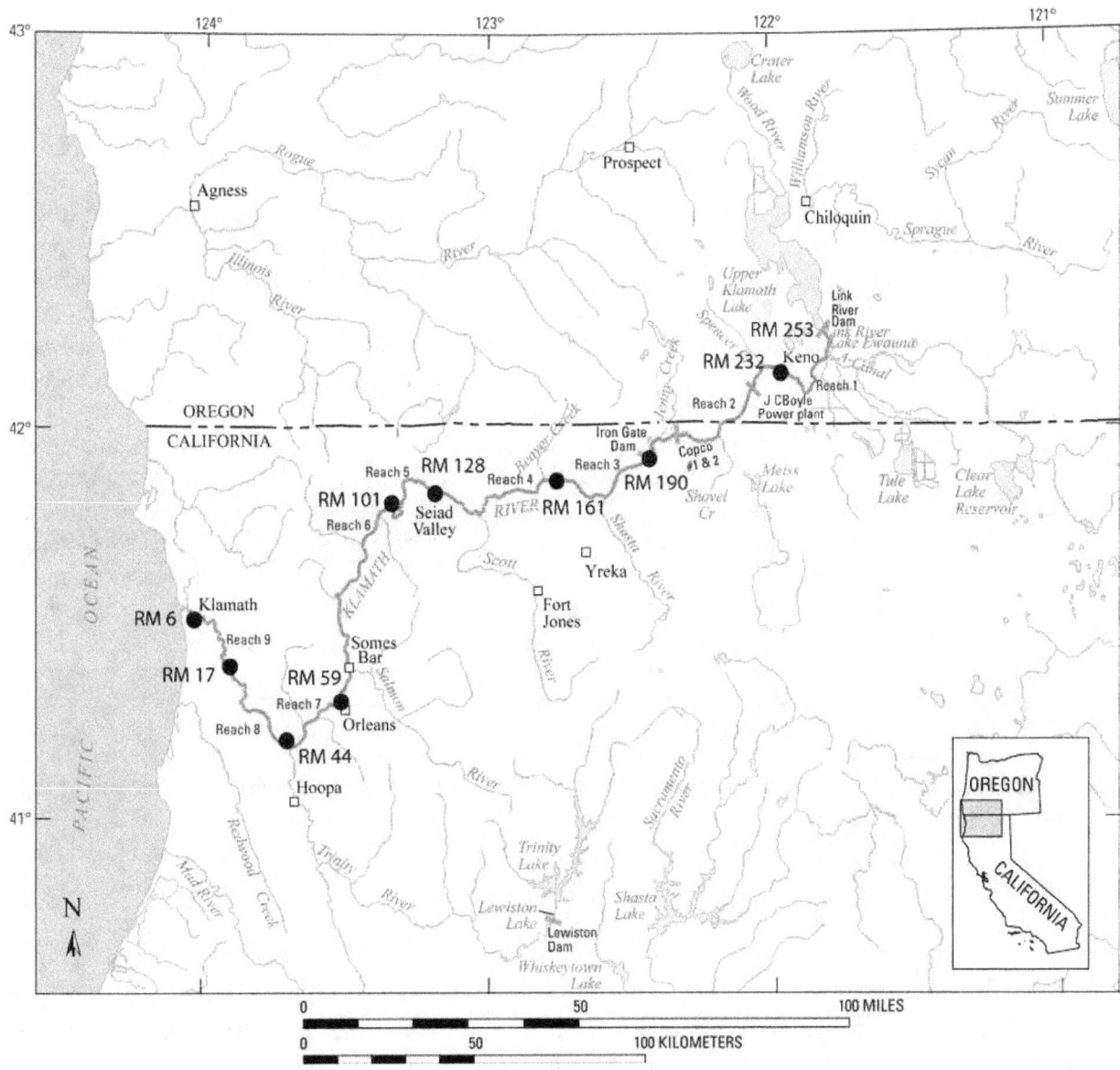

Figure 1. Map of the Klamath River showing the study area from Link River Dam to the Pacific Ocean. Points (•) mark locations with observed temperature data (RM = river mile) used for calibration and for separating the river into nine model reaches.

5

Methods

Structure of RBM10

RBM10 is a 1-dimensional water temperature model based on a heat budget formulation to predict daily water temperatures along the longitudinal profile of a river (Yearsley and others, 2001; Yearsley, 2009). The model's structure and associated input files can be separated into three components: (1) river geometry, (2) boundary conditions, and (3) meteorological data. The model defines system geometry as a series of either reservoir or river segments. Each segment is defined by simple continuity equations that dictate how properties such as width, depth, and water velocity change with river discharge. Boundary conditions consist of heat advected into the mainstem river from headwaters and tributaries, and must be specified as daily inputs of discharge and temperature for each source. Given boundary conditions and river geometry, RBM10 uses a simple equilibrium flow model, assuming discharge in each river segment on each day is transmitted downstream instantaneously. Inputs for the heat budget are calculated daily from standard meteorological data. Water temperatures are then simulated using a mixed Eulerian-Lagrangian numerical scheme that is both accurate and computationally efficient (Yearsley, 2009). Below, we describe in detail how we structured RBM10 for the Klamath River. First, we describe the simulation of historical water temperatures, which includes calibration and validation against observed temperature data. We then use the calibrated model to predict water temperatures under management alternatives and climate scenarios.

Reconstruction of Historical Daily Water Temperature

Our goal was to reconstruct a 50-year historical time series of water temperature in the Klamath River that could be used as a baseline against which to compare simulations of management alternatives and climate scenarios. In addition, simulating a long time series allowed us to take advantage of observed water temperatures dating back to 1962 for model calibration. We compiled input data that allowed us to reconstruct a 49-year historical time series extending from January 1, 1961, to September 30, 2009, from Link River at RM 253.0 to RM 5.7 near the Pacific Ocean.

River Geometry

To model the hydraulic properties of the Klamath River, the geometry of the river was defined as a series of segments with unique attributes such as cross-sectional area and wetted channel width. RBM10 defines river geometry differently for reservoir and river segments. Reservoir segments are assumed to have a constant water surface elevation, and each segment's geometry is defined in terms of its volume (acre-feet) and surface area (square feet) computed at mean operating pool elevation. The geometry of river segments is characterized by wetted channel width and cross-sectional area, both of which vary with river discharge. Continuity equations were used to quantify these relationships:

$$W_x = a_W Q^{b_W},$$
(1)

$$A_x = a_A Q^{b_A},$$
(2)

where W_x and A_x are wetted top width (feet) and cross-sectional area (square feet), respectively, for the segment beginning at river mile x, Q is discharge (cubic feet per second), and a and b are segment-specific parameters that need to be estimated.

We used several existing models to construct a continuous river geometry from Link River Dam to the ocean (table 1). Reservoir segments in CE-QUAL-W2 (A. Sullivan, U.S. Geological Survey, written commun., 2011) and HEC-RAS (U.S. Army Corps of Engineers, 2010) were aggregated to estimate surface area and volume of segments approximately 0.6 mi long (tables A1 and A2). For river segments, we used HEC-RAS (U.S. Army Corps of Engineers, 2010) parameterized by the Reclamation for the Klamath River to estimate the parameters of the continuity equations (eqs. 1 and 2). For the lowest 100 mi of river, nine channel cross sections were incorporated into the HEC-RAS model. These cross sections were obtained from the HEC-5Q model (U.S. Army Corps of Engineers, 1987) constructed for the Klamath River (Bartholow and others, 2005).

Table 1. Data sources used for defining channel geometry of the Klamath River.

River section	River mile (start - end)	Model	Data source
Lake Ewauna to Keno Dam	253.0 - 233.4	CE-QUAL-W2	Sullivan, 2011
Keno Dam to Clear Creek	233.4 - 98.6	HEC-RAS	Greimann and others, 2011
Clear Creek to Pacific Ocean	98.6 - 0.0	HEC-5Q	Bartholow and others, 2005

To quantify wetted top-width and cross-sectional area as a function of discharge, first we ran HEC-RAS at 13 levels of discharge ranging from 600 to 12,000 ft^3/s. This provided estimates of top width and cross-sectional area at each level of discharge for 1,193 channel cross sections. Next, we divided river sections into segments of relatively constant slope resulting in river segments for RBM10 averaging 8 mi long (range = 0.5–32.6 mi long; tables A1 and A2). For each discharge level, we then averaged the wetted width and area over all cross sections within a given segment. Finally, for each segment, we estimated a_W, b_W, a_A, and b_A by fitting a linear regression of the form $\ln(y) = \ln a + b \ln Q$ (tables A1 and A2). Overall, 85 reservoir and river segments were used to characterize the geometry of the Klamath River (table A1).

Meteorological Data

RBM10 uses a heat budget formulation to quantify heat flux at the air water interface (Yearsley and others, 2001; Yearsley, 2009):

$$H_{\text{air-water}} = (H_{\text{sw}} - H_{\text{rs}}) + (H_a - H_{\text{ar}}) + H_{\text{evap}} + H_{\text{cond}} + H_{\text{back}}, \qquad (3)$$

where $H_{\text{air-water}}$ is the net exchange of thermal energy across the air-water interface, H_{sw} is shortwave solar radiation incident at the water's surface, H_{rs} is reflected shortwave solar radiation, H_a is longwave atmospheric radiation incident at the water surface, H_{ar} is reflected longwave atmospheric radiation, H_{evap} is evaporative heat flux, H_{cond} is conductive heat flux, and H_{back} is longwave back radiation from the water surface. All terms are in units of kilocalories per meter squared per second.

Standard meteorological data are used to quantify $H_{air\text{-}water}$. Net shortwave solar radiation (H_{sw} - H_{rs}) and net longwave atmospheric radiation (H_a - H_{ar}) are direct inputs to the model, whereas the remaining terms in the heat budget are calculated by RBM10 from inputs of daily-mean air temperature (°C), daily-mean wind speed (meters per second) vapor pressure (milibar), and a psychrometric constant needed to calculate the Bowen ratio (Yearsley, 2001). In addition, although not a direct model input, cloud cover is required to calculate net shortwave and longwave radiation. Meteorological inputs to RBM10 are spatially explicit, allowing the model to account for the substantial gradient in climate as the Klamath River traverses from headwaters to ocean. We created nine model reaches, each having a unique set of meteorological input data, based primarily on the availability of sites with a sufficient record of water temperature measurements for use in model calibration and validation (tables A1 and A2). Reaches varied in length from 10.8 to 42.4 mi.

Long time series of meteorological data from weather stations along the Klamath River are limited. Therefore, we constructed model inputs from simulated meteorological data, allowing us to develop a 49-year historical record of meteorology. Simulated meteorological data included maximum and minimum air temperature and cloud cover, by river mile, for 1961–2008 (supplied courtesy of Lorraine Flint, U.S. Geological Survey). Methods to simulate air temperature and cloud cover are described in Flint and Flint (2008). Air temperature and cloud cover data for the river mile at the midpoint of each reach were used in RBM10. The cloud cover dataset was extended through 2009 using the long-term mean of cloud cover for a given Julian day. Daily mean air temperature was estimated as the mean of minimum and maximum daily air temperatures. Local measured air temperature data were used to extend the simulated air temperature dataset through 2009. Measured values were adjusted up or down by a fixed amount to visually match simulated temperatures; adjustments ranged from -2° to 1°C for daily-mean air temperature, and -3° to 1°C for daily-minimum air temperature, depending on reach. Daily-mean wind speed (1961–2009) was obtained from a simulated 1/8-degree gridded meteorological dataset of the continental United States (Maurer and others, 2002; University of Washington, 2011). Grid locations closest to the latitude and longitude of the midpoint of each reach were used in RBM10.

Shortwave solar radiation incident at the water surface (H_{sw}) was estimated by calculating solar radiation at the top of the atmosphere and then adjusting for cloud cover (Henderson-Sellers, 1986):

$$H_{sw} = H_\infty(A + B(1\text{-}c)), \tag{4}$$

where H_∞ is shortwave solar radiation incident at the top of the atmosphere, c is cloud cover represented as the fraction of sky covered with clouds, and A and B are coefficients. Top-of-the-atmosphere radiation was calculated from latitude and Julian day using methods described in Henderson-Sellers (1986). We estimated A and B using cloud cover estimates for reach 1 from Flint and Flint (2008) and measured solar radiation for 2002–08 from an AgriMet weather station at Worden, Oreg. (AgriMet, 2011; available: *http://www.usbr.gov/pn/agrimet/agrimetmap/wrdoda.html*). To estimate A and B, we used an optimization routine to minimize the sum of absolute deviations between observed and predicted solar radiation ($\hat{A}$ = 0.131, $\hat{B}$ = 0.619, R^2 = 0.853, fig. 2). These parameter estimates were then used to estimate solar radiation for all reaches using reach-specific latitude and cloud cover. Reflected shortwave solar radiation was calculated as $H_{rs} = H_{sw}A_{sw}$, where A_{sw} is the shortwave reflectivity of the water surface. Shortwave reflectivity was calculated from latitude, Julian day, and cloud cover using methods described in Henderson-Sellers (1986).

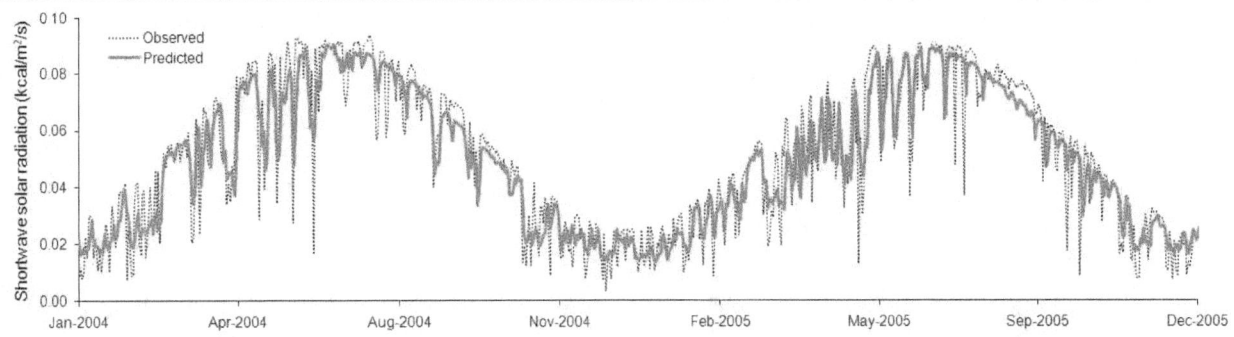

Figure 2. Comparison of observed shortwave solar radiation at Worden, Oregon, to predicted shortwave solar radiation for 2004–05.

Longwave atmospheric radiation incident at the water surface was calculated using the Stefan-Boltzmann law:

$$H_a = \varepsilon_{eff} \sigma T_a^4,$$ (5)

where ε_{eff} is the effective emissivity of the atmosphere, σ is the Stefan-Boltzmann constant, and T_a is daily-mean air temperature (K). We used models for ε_{eff} recommended by Flerchinger and others (2009), who compared estimates from different algorithms for longwave radiation to measured longwave radiation at 21 sites across North American and China. Specifically, we calculated clear-sky emissivity, ε_{clr}, using the model of Ångström (1918):

$$\varepsilon_{clr} = 0.83 - 0.18 \times 10^{-0.067 e_a},$$ (6)

where e_a is vapor pressure (kilopascal). Effective emissivity was then calculated by adjusting clear-sky emissivity for cloud cover using the model of Unsworth and Monteith (1975):

$$\varepsilon_{eff} = \left(1 - 0.84c\right)\varepsilon_{clr} + 0.84c .$$ (7)

Reflected longwave radiation was calculated as $H_{ar} = H_a A_{ar}$, where A_{ar} is longwave reflectivity, which was set to 0.03.

Vapor pressure (e_a) typically is calculated from either relative humidity or dew point temperature, neither of which was available to us. Instead, we estimated vapor pressure from minimum air temperature using an exponential relation fit to minimum air temperature and vapor pressure from observed meteorological data from the Worden, Oregon Agrimet Station for 2000–10 (used for reaches 1–7) and from Arcata, California for 1992–93 (used for reaches 8 and 9; available: *http://www.ncdc.noaa.gov/oa/ncdc.html*; fig. 3).

All other components of the heat budget were calculated as described by Yearsley and others (2001), although it is useful to repeat the formulation of the evaporative heat flux since this term contains parameters required to calibrate RBM10:

$$H_{evap} = \rho L_v f(W)(e_o - e_a),$$ (8)

where ρ is the density of water (kilograms per meter cubed), L_v is the latent heat of vaporization (kilocalories per kilogram), $f(W)$ is a function of wind speed (W), and e_0 is the saturation vapor pressure at the temperature of the water surface (milibar). The wind speed function often takes the general form:

$$f(W) = a + bW + cW^2,\qquad\qquad(9)$$

where a, b, and c are empirical coefficients (Edinger and others, 1974). The specific form of $f(W)$ varies widely among studies (Edinger and others, 1974; Henderson-Sellers, 1986). For example, Yearsley and others (2001) used the simplest form for $f(W)$, assuming $a = 0$ and $c = 0$; they then estimated b through calibration. Coefficients of the wind speed function are the only calibration parameters in RBM10 (see section, "Calibration and Validation").

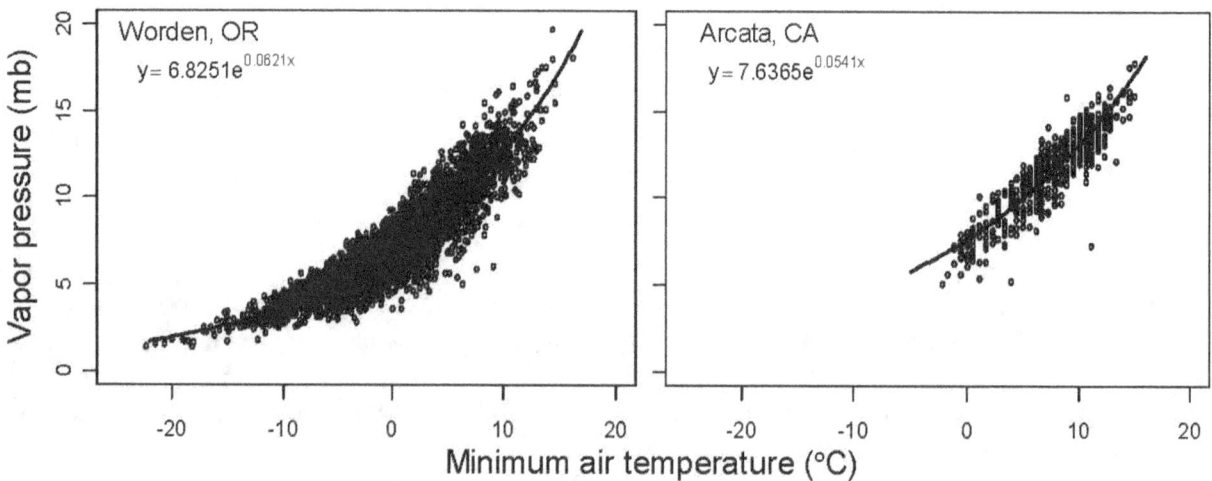

Figure 3. Vapor pressure versus minimum air temperature at Worden, Oregon, and Arcata, California. Best-fit exponential relationship between minimum air temperature and vapor pressure also is shown (R^2 = 0.843 for Worden, Oregon; R^2 = 0.805 for Arcata, California).

Boundary Conditions

Daily values of river discharge and water temperature must be provided at all boundaries where significant discharge enters the mainstem Klamath River. We included the following tributaries as boundary conditions to RBM10: Link River, creeks and irrigation canal return flows into Lake Ewauna, Spencer Creek, Shovel Creek, Jenny Creek, Boyle Springs, Shasta River, Scott River, Salmon River, and Trinity River (tables A1 and A2).

Daily-mean streamflow data for the USGS gage below Link River Dam (station 11507500) and estimated monthly westside Keno Canal flows were used as the upstream boundary to the water-temperature model. Specifically, for water years 1961–83, we used published USGS daily flows for the westside Keno Canal. The USGS gage for the westside Keno Canal was not operated after 1983. Thus, for water years 1984–2010, we used monthly-mean canal flows, which were estimated from a flow versus power generation rating curve. The monthly flows were not disaggregated, and were simply added to the daily-mean flows measured at the USGS river gage to obtain a total flow for Link River. This seemed justified since historically, the Keno canal flows have only been about 10 percent of the total flow.

All other boundary conditions were specified using estimates of historical daily discharge and accretions constructed by the Reclamation for their Secretarial Determination analysis (Greimann and others, 2011). An aggregate measure of canal flows into Lake Ewauna was estimated as the difference in daily discharge between the USGS gage below Keno Dam and the Link River upstream boundary. With the exception of Boyle Springs and Jenny Creek, tributary flows were estimated as the accretion between given control points along the Klamath River. Boyle Springs was set at a constant discharge of 225 ft^3/s (PacifiCorp, 2004) and temperature of 11.3°C (Turaski, 2003). To balance flows at Iron Gate Dam, discharge for Jenny Creek was computed as difference between Iron Gate flows and the sum of Boyle Springs flow and flow just upstream of Jenny Creek. Tributary inputs could be either positive or negative because they were formed from accretions that balance both inflows (via groundwater, tributaries, and canals) and outflows (via infiltration, evaporation, or canal diversion).

We assembled time series of observed daily water temperature for each boundary in our model (table 2); however, a complete time series was not available (fig. 4). To fill data gaps in the 49-year time series, we used a regression model that predicts weekly-mean stream temperature as a function of weekly-mean air temperature (Mohseni and others, 1998):

$$T_s = \mu + \frac{\alpha - \mu}{1 + e^{\gamma(\beta - T_a)}} , \qquad (10)$$

where T_s is the weekly-mean stream temperature, μ is the minimum water temperature, α is the maximum water temperature, β is the air temperature at the point of inflection, γ represents the slope at the inflection point, and T_a is the weekly-mean air temperature (°C). The parameter μ was set to 0°C and then α, β, and γ were estimated by least squares using an optimization routine in the R statistical package (R Development Core Team, 2010). Weekly-mean air temperatures for a tributary entering a given model reach were computed from the daily-mean air temperatures of that reach. Following Mohseni and others (1998), we fit separate relationships to the rising and falling limb (that is, the part of the year when air temperature tends to increase or decrease; figs. 5 and 6). Given parameter estimates for the rising and falling limb of each stream (table 3), we then filled data gaps by predicting daily water temperature using a 7-day moving average of air temperature.

Table 2. Source of input datasets for statistical models used to estimate boundary water temperatures.

Tributary	Period	Source	Station ID	Latitude	Longitude
Link Dam	2001–2010	USGS/BOR	11507500	42.22	121.79
Klamath Straits Drain	1968–2010	ODEQ	10763	42.08	121.84
Spencer Creek	1999–2004	Flint and Flint (2008)	—	—	—
Shovel Creek	2001–2004	Flint and Flint (2008)	—	—	—
Jenny Creek	2001–2004	Flint and Flint (2008)	—	—	—
Shasta River	2001–2010	USFWS	SHKR1	41.83	122.59
Scott River	2001-2010	USFWS	SCKR1	41.77	123.02
Salmon River	2002–2007	USFWS	SAKR1	41.38	123.48
Trinity River	2002–2010	USFWS	TRWE1	41.18	123.70

Most sources of water temperature data included time periods of continuously measured water temperature (fig. 4), but measured water temperature data for flows entering Lake Ewauna between Link River Dam and Keno Dam are limited. However, a total of 229 point samples of water temperature have been intermittently collected by Oregon Department of Environmental Quality (ODEQ) since 1968 in the Klamath Straits Drain (available: *http://www.deq.state.or.us/wq/assessment/ rpt0406/results.asp*). These data were used to estimate weekly-mean water temperature of inflows to Lake Ewauna.

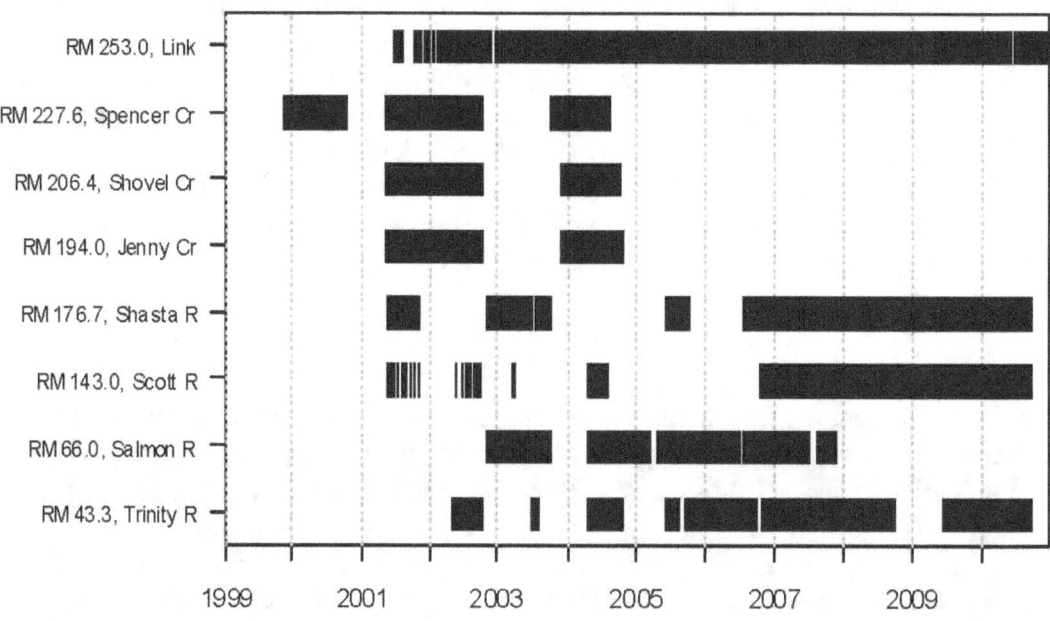

Figure 4. Extent of measured water temperature data for tributary inputs to the Klamath River (RM = river mile). Black horizontal bars represent the range of available data for each tributary. Data for Klamath Straits Drain is excluded from this plot due to lack of a continuous water temperature record.

Table 3. Parameter estimates of the non-linear regression model (Mohseni and others, 1998) used to estimate water temperature for headwater and tributary inputs.

Tributary	Model reach	Limb	First week of limb	$\hat{\alpha}$	$\hat{\beta}$	$\hat{\gamma}$
Link Dam	1	rising	52	24.5	8.5	0.215
		falling	30	24.9	9.5	0.201
Canals	1	rising	52	26.7	8.3	0.213
		falling	30	27.4	10.1	0.170
Spencer Creek	2	rising	52	19.7	10.2	0.339
		falling	30	23.6	15.3	0.184
Shovel Creek	2	rising	52	17.6	9.9	0.165
		falling	30	21.8	13.3	0.092
Jenny Creek	2	rising	52	21.4	9.7	0.242
		falling	30	24.5	12.7	0.135
Shasta River	3	rising	1	27.3	10.1	0.149
		falling	31	36.3	18.1	0.107
Scott River	4	rising	52	24.7	11.9	0.157
		falling	31	25.1	12.1	0.165
Salmon River	6	rising	52	24.7	14.2	0.188
		falling	30	27.9	16.3	0.160
Trinity River	8	rising	52	25.1	11.6	0.186
		falling	32	24.3	10.7	0.189

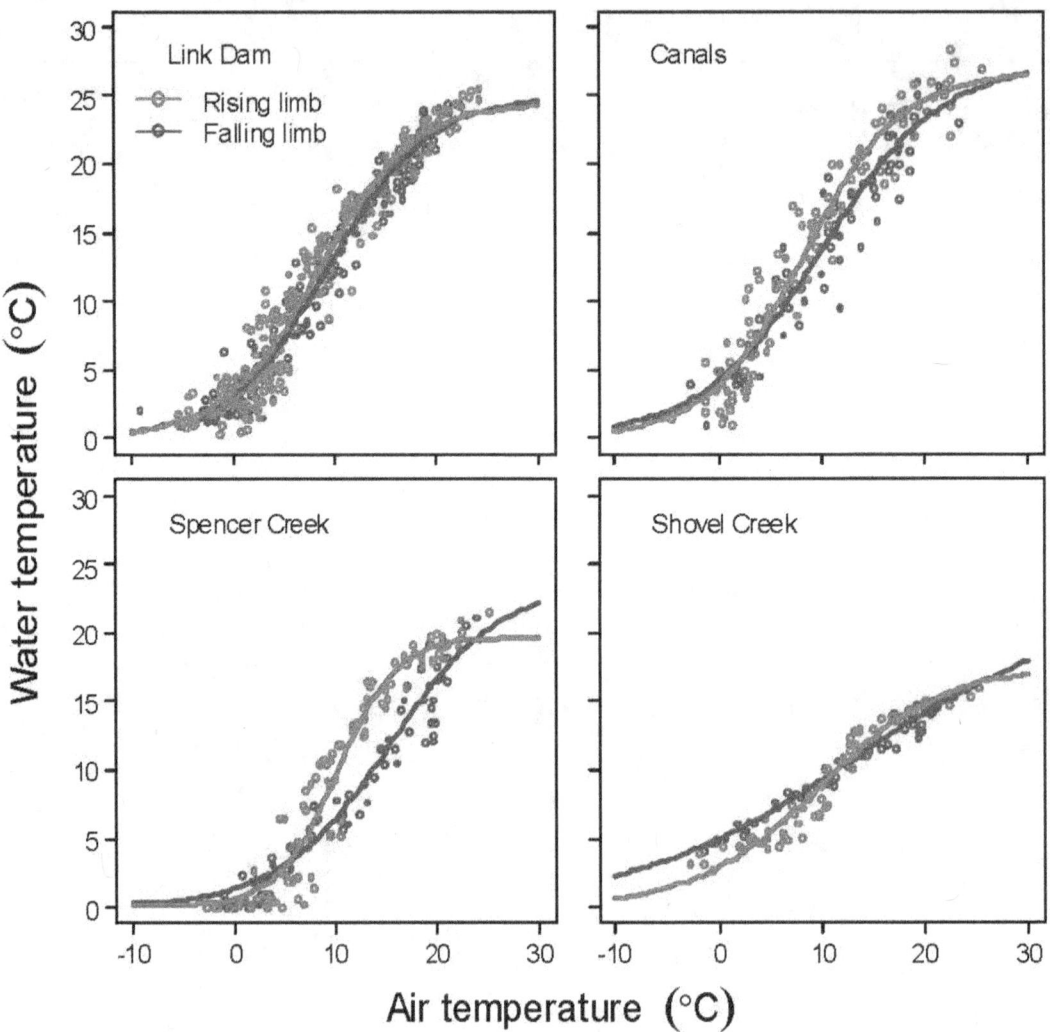

Figure 5. Scatter plots of observed weekly mean water temperature against weekly mean air temperature for four headwater and tributary inputs. Two lines in each panel represent the fitted non-linear regression model (Mohseni and others, 1998) used to predict water temperatures for the rising and falling limbs of air temperature.

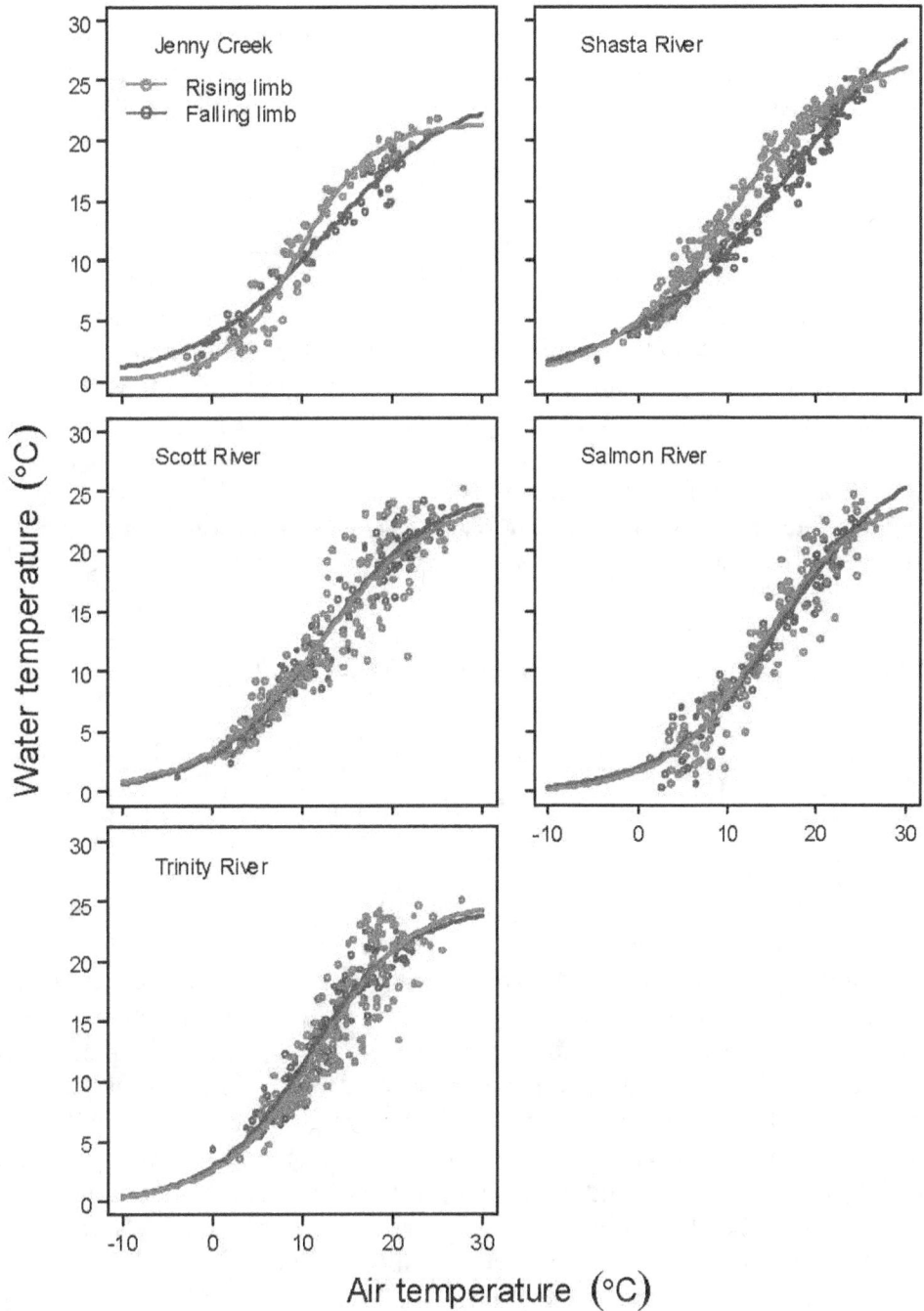

Figure 6. Scatter plots of observed weekly mean water temperature against weekly mean air temperature for five tributary inputs. Two lines in each panel represent the fitted non-linear regression model (Mohseni and others, 1998) used to predict water temperatures for the rising and falling limbs of air temperature.

Calibration and Validation

The only calibration parameters in RBM10 are coefficients that influence how wind speed affects evaporative heat flux. Heat lost through evaporation is proportional to the wind speed function, $f(W)$, and to the vapor pressure deficit, e_o-e_a (eq. 8). We assessed the fit of the water temperature model to observed data using two forms of the wind function. First, we used a common form of the wind speed function,

$$f(W_r) = a_r + b_r W_r, \tag{11}$$

where r is reach 1,…, 9 corresponding to each unique set of meteorological data. Observed temperatures at nine locations along the river were close to the break points for each reach (fig. 7, tables A1 and A2), providing a direct correspondence among observed water temperature data, meteorological data, and wind-function parameters. To calibrate the model, we used an optimization routine to find parameter values of a_r and b_r that minimized the sum of squared deviations between predicted and observed temperatures. We calibrated one reach at a time, from upstream to downstream, because water temperatures at the end of reach r form the boundary conditions at the start of reach $r+1$. For example, observed water temperatures at the end of reach 1 were used to estimate a_1 and b_1. Next, a_1 and b_1 were set to their best-fit values and observed water temperatures at the end of reach 2 were used to estimate a_2 and b_2, and so on.

We also calibrated the water temperature model using a wind speed function with seasonal evaporation coefficients similar to the approach of Deas and Orlob (1999):

$$f\left(W_r\right) = \begin{cases} a_{r,1} + b_{r,1} W_r & \text{if April 1} \leq d \leq \text{November 1} \\ a_{r,2} + b_{r,2} W_r & \text{if November 1} < d < \text{April 1} \end{cases} \tag{12}$$

Where d is the day of year and $a_{r,j}$ and $b_{r,j}$, ($j = \{1,2\}$) are coefficients that apply to either the period April 1 to November 1 ("summer") or November 1 to April 1 ("winter").

All available data were used for calibration so that parameters were estimated across a wide range of annual variation in weather and hydrology. We assembled an extensive dataset comprised of more than 42,000 observations of daily-mean water temperatures, with four sites having more than 25 years of data (fig. 7). Measured water temperature data were acquired from the U.S. Geological Survey National Water Information System (USGS NWIS) website; Sharon Campbell, U.S. Geological Survey, Fort Collins, Colorado; Jessica Asbill, Reclamation, Klamath Falls, Oregon; Paul Zedonis, U.S. Fish and Wildlife Service, Arcata, California; and Carolyn Cook, U.S. Forest Service (USFS) Six Rivers National Forest, Eureka, California. Water temperature data from the USGS and the other agencies were measured hourly and needed to be averaged to daily-mean values.

We used both statistical and graphical methods to judge model fit and to compare the two models with different wind functions (eqs. 11 and 12). Goodness-of-fit statistics included the root mean square error (RMSE), mean error (ME), absolute mean error (AME), and the Nash-Sutcliffe statistic (NSS). To assess systematic departures of the model, we plotted observed versus expected water temperatures and residuals versus observed water temperatures. We compared model fit between wind functions and then selected the wind function that yielded the minimum bias and error for use in all subsequent water temperature simulations.

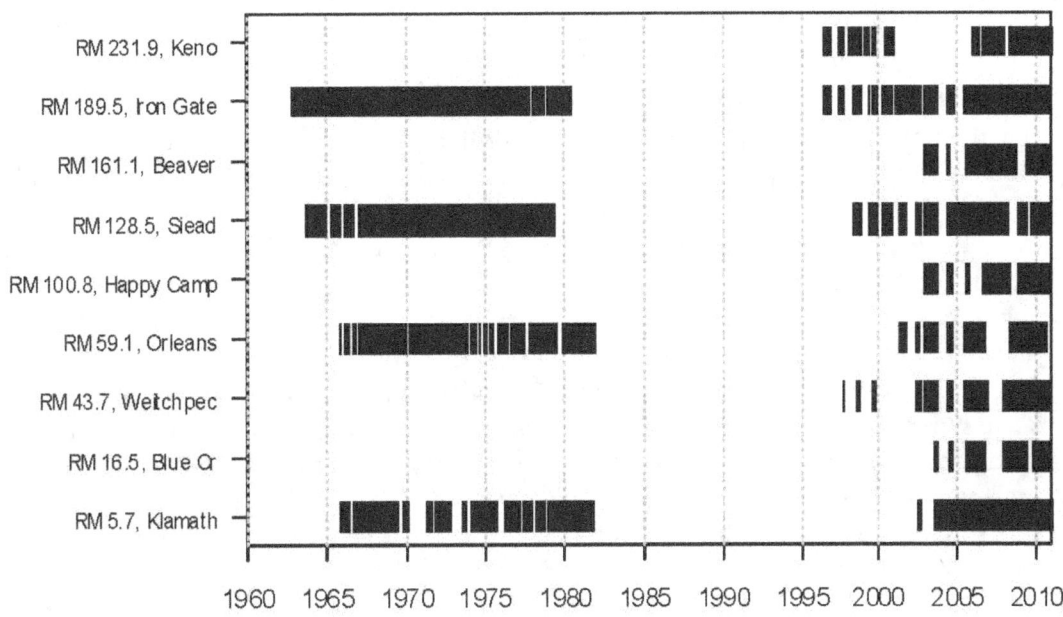

Figure 7. Extent of observed water temperature data at nine locations used for calibration and validation of RBM10 (RM = river mile). Black bars represent the range of available data for each reach.

To evaluate model predictions against data not used to fit the model, we used k-fold cross validation (Davison and Hinkley, 1997). This technique involves: (1) splitting the calibration dataset into k = 1,..., K subsets, (2) leaving out the kth subset (the "assessment set") while the remaining data are used to estimate the parameters (the "training set"), and then (3) using parameter estimates from the training set to predict water temperatures for the assessment set. This process is repeated for all K subsets, goodness-of-fit statistics for each assessment set are calculated, and then an aggregate measure of fit is calculated as the mean of a particular statistic over all subsets.

For our cross-validation, we split the calibration dataset into subsets by reach and year and conducted a cross-validation for each reach. The best-fit parameters estimated during the calibration process were used as initial values. As described above, we then set aside observed data from year k in reach r, used the remaining data to estimate $a_{r,-k}$ and $b_{r,-k}$ (where -k indicates exclusion of the kth year), and then predicted water temperatures for year k in reach r using estimates of $a_{r,-k}$ and $b_{r,-k}$. Because the K subsets were unequal in size due to missing data in some years, we used a weighted average of the goodness-of-fit statistics with weights equal to the fraction of the observations in the kth year.

Simulating Management Alternatives and Climate Scenarios

We used RBM10 to simulate water temperatures for 2012–2061 under two management alternatives and six future climate scenarios (that is, twelve 50-year simulations). The two management alternatives are referred to as: (1) BO, which represents the no action alternative, and (2) KBRA, which represents the action alternative to remove the four lower dams on the Klamath River (J.C. Boyle, Copco 1, Copco 2, and Iron Gate) in addition to the KBRA actions and restoration programs. Under the no action alternative (BO), dams remain in place for the entire 50-year simulation period (2012–2061), and simulated flows are subject to the 2010 biological opinion (National Marine Fisheries Service, 2010). For the KBRA alternative, dams remain in place through 2019 and for modeling purposes, are assumed to be removed instantaneously on January 1, 2020. For the KBRA alternative, river flows were simulated under the expected flow management of the KBRA. Total Maximum Daily Loads or other regulatory processes that might reduce future water temperatures were not included in the simulations.

The six future climate scenarios represent hydrology and meteorology using the "Index Sequential Method" and five alternative Global Circulation Models (GCMs) (Greimann and others, 2011). The Index Sequential Method simulates future operational conditions using historical hydrology and meteorology (Greimann and others, 2011). That is, the Index Sequential Method uses historical hydrology and meteorology data applied to the proposed flow operational conditions of either BO or KBRA. A 50-year record of hydrology and meteorology was constructed using 1961–2009 data for 2012–2060 (49 years), and 1961 data were then repeated for the 50th year (2061). In contrast, scenarios run under the five GCM models incorporate both the effects of climate change and management alternatives. The hydrologic models used to predict the five climate change scenarios were adapted from those described in a recent report for the Secretary's Determination on Klamath River Dam Removal and Basin Restoration by Greimann and others (2011), and used in two previous studies (U.S. Department of the Interior, 2008, 2009). Particular GCMs were selected based on their quantile rankings of predicted temperature and precipitation change [table 4; see Greimann and others (2011) and King and others (2011) for details]. As shown in table 4, the GCMs with the highest (CCCMA) and lowest (NCAR) temperature and precipitation quantile rankings predicted higher and lower magnitudes of future temperature and precipitation change, respectively. Two other GCMs were selected based on highest precipitation and lowest temperature (MRI) and highest temperature and lowest precipitation (MIUB) quantile rankings, respectively. A fifth GCM (GFDL) was selected because it had both a median precipitation and temperature ranking.

We used RBM10, as calibrated to historical data, to simulate mean daily water temperatures under each of the climate scenarios and management alternatives. Hydrology and river geometry were based on analyses of Greimann and others (2011), meteorology was based on a combination of historical data and GCM air temperatures, and water temperatures for boundary conditions (that is, tributaries) were simulated from projected air temperatures. Further details on model structure for these simulations are described below.

Table 4. Description for Global Circulation Models (GCMs) selected by Greimann and others (2011) for constructing future hydrology under the no action (BO) and action (KBRA) alternatives.

Model	Description	Temperature quantile	Precipitation quantile
CCCMA	Canadian Centre for Climate Modeling Analysis	75th	75th
GFDL	Geophysical Fluid Dynamics Laboratory	50th	50th
MIUB	Meteorological Institute of the University of Bonn	75th	25th
MRI	Meteorological Research Institute	25th	75th
NCAR	National Center for Atmospheric Research	25th	25th

Our comparison of these scenarios focused first on understanding the effects of each management alternative on water temperatures in the absence of climate change. For this purpose, we focused on the Index Sequential Method climate scenario, which used historical hydrology and meteorology under BO (no action alternative) or KBRA (action alternative) management alternatives. We summarized simulation results by dividing the simulation into two periods (2012–2019 and 2020–2061), allowing comparison between alternatives when dams are in place for both KBRA and BO (2012–2019) relative to the latter period (2020–2061) when dams are removed under KBRA but remain in place under the BO alternative. In addition, we included the historical simulation as a baseline against which to compare the various management and climate scenarios.

River Geometry

River geometry for simulations with dams was the same as that used for the historical simulation described above. For the KBRA alternative after dam removal, we used a HEC-RAS model for a free-flowing Klamath River between Keno Dam and Iron Gate Dam, as parameterized by Reclamation (Greimann and others, 2011). We converted reservoir segments to river segments and then estimated parameters of the continuity equations required by RBM10 as described previously (table A2).

Meteorological Data

Meteorological inputs for the Index Sequential Method scenario (2012–2061) were identical to the input data set for the historical period (1961–2009), except for water year 2010 data, which was constructed with data from water year 1961. Because the pattern of leap years for 2012–2061 did not match the historical period, the two time periods were offset by 1 day for some years. Therefore, data for February 28 was repeated on February 29 for leap years.

For the climate change scenarios, three sets of daily-mean air temperatures (1951–2099), temporally downscaled from monthly-mean air temperatures for each of the five GCMs (CCCMA, GDFL, MIUB, MRI, NCAR), were compiled by the Bureau of Reclamation (Blair Greimann, Bureau of Reclamation, Denver, Colo., written commun., 2010). The three datasets included the upper Klamath Basin (upstream of Iron Gate Dam), lower Klamath Basin (downstream of Iron Gate Dam), and a subbasin of the lower Klamath Basin near the ocean. The upper Klamath and lower Klamath basin sets were applied to meteorological reaches 1–2 and reaches 3–7, respectively. The lower Klamath subbasin set was applied to reaches 8–9.

Temporal downscaling was necessary because the GCMs predicted future air temperature and precipitation on a monthly basis and the water temperature model required input data on a daily basis. To create synthetic time series of daily values for the future time period (2012–2061), King and others (2011) created sets of "scaling dates" which were specified months from the 1961–2008 historic period that was reassigned to the future period. The sets of "scaling dates" were specific to each GCM and the upper and lower Klamath basins (The coastal KCLM1 subbasin used the same scaling dates as the lower Klamath Basin). The sequence of months from the historical period as defined by the scaling date was not necessarily consecutive. For example, the CCCMA model used historical period daily data from February 1982 for January 2024, for the lower basin reaches. However, for the following month of the same simulation (February 2024), this model used historical period daily data from November 1966.

Bias-corrections to five GCM daily-mean air temperature sets were required because GCMs typically under- or over-predict observed historical temperatures when used to simulate past climate conditions. Bias-corrections (ΔT) brought mean GCM air temperatures closer to local climate conditions along the Klamath River, but did not alter daily variation in temperature. Optimal ΔT values for each of the nine model reaches were determined using the mean of the annual-mean air temperatures of the five GCMs and the historical (1961–2010) annual-mean air temperatures based on PRISM data downscaled to a local spatial resolution (Daly and others, 2008; Flint and Flint, 2008). Thus, for each of the nine reaches, the same value of ΔT was used for all five GCMs. The optimal ΔT was identified by minimizing the difference between the mean of the bias-corrected annual-mean air temperature and the historical period annual-mean air temperature. This procedure resulted in the lowest root mean square error and a Nash-Sutcliffe statistic that was closest to zero (table 5, fig. 8). The optimal ΔT for each model reach was then applied to the GCM air temperature data sets for the simulation period 2012–2061. For example, increasing the annual-mean air temperatures from the GCMs by 2.53°C in reach 1 was required to minimize the difference between observed historical and GCM mean annual air temperatures (table 5). This increase in air temperature was then applied to the all daily GCM air temperatures for 2012–2061 to construct the meteorological dataset for reach 1.

Table 5. Bias corrections (ΔT) to annual mean air temperatures from General Circulation Model (GCM) used in simulations of Klamath River water temperatures with RBM10.

[NSS = Nash-Sutcliffe statistic, RMSE = root mean square error]

Model reach	ΔT (°C)	GCM dataset	NSS	RMSE
1	2.53	Upper Klamath	-0.0758	0.6315
2	3.22	Upper Klamath	0.3974	0.5760
3	2.16	Lower Klamath	-0.0676	0.5960
4	2.47	Lower Klamath	-0.2634	0.9898
5	3.54	Lower Klamath	-0.1484	0.5620
6	4.40	Lower Klamath	-7.7578	1.4636
7	4.34	Lower Klamath	0.3895	0.4706
8	2.08	Lower Klamath	-0.0901	0.6160
9	2.02	Lower Klamath	-0.0508	0.4906

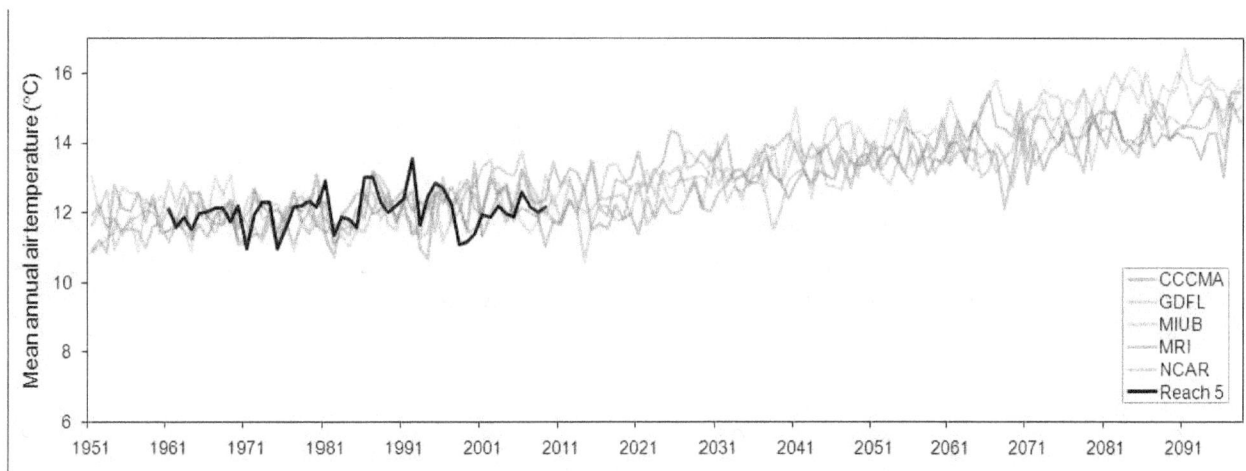

Figure 8. Comparison of mean annual air temperature in model reach 5 to bias-corrected GCM air temperatures for reach 5 based on GCM model output for the lower Klamath Basin.

Remaining meteorological inputs needed for the climate change simulations included shortwave solar radiation, longwave atmospheric radiation, wind speed, and vapor pressure. Although not used directly by the water-temperature model, cloud cover and minimum air temperature data were needed to compute shortwave radiation, longwave radiation, and vapor pressure. Wind speed and cloud cover data from the historical period [water year (WY) 1961–2010] simulations were used to construct daily time series for the GCM time period (WY 2011–2061). The sequence of historical data used in the GCM time period was based on temporal "scaling dates" described previously.

To estimate daily-minimum air temperatures the difference between the daily mean and daily minimum air temperature (from the historical period: 1961–2010) was computed for each day for all nine reaches. The average of these daily differences was then computed by month over the entire period (1961–2010). We then applied a 30-day moving average to compute the difference between mean and minimum air temperature for each Julian day. New daily time series for each model reach were created for the GCM period (WY 2011–2061) based on a 30-day average smoothing of the monthly air temperature difference values. These daily air temperature differences were then subtracted from the daily-mean air temperatures of each GCM to estimate the daily-minimum air temperature.

Given estimates of cloud cover, mean air temperature, and minimum air temperature; net shortwave radiation, net longwave radiation, and vapor pressure were computed using methods described in the previous section.

Boundary Conditions

Daily flows and accretions under the Index Sequential Method and GCM models were obtained from Reclamation as used in the analysis by Greimann and others (2011). We constructed boundary inflows to the mainstem Klamath River from the simulated hydrology as described above for the historical simulation. Daily water temperatures entering the mainstem via headwaters and tributaries were simulated by using air temperatures from the Index Sequential Method and GCM models in the regression models of Mohseni and others (1998). Because the regression models were parameterized to historical data from the tributaries (table 3), this simulation assumes the relationship between weekly mean air temperature and weekly-mean water temperature will not change in the future.

Results

Historical Simulation

Based on measures of both precision and bias, we selected the wind function with seasonal evaporation coefficients (eq. 12) for simulating water temperatures of the Klamath River. For every reach, measures of precision (RMSE and MAE) were smaller for the model with seasonal evaporation coefficients (table 7) compared to the model with constant evaporation coefficients (table 6). Furthermore, bias (as measured by the mean error) was smaller for the model with seasonal evaporation coefficients (tables 6 and 7). For the model with seasonal evaporation coefficients, the residuals as a function of water temperature revealed no consistent bias for reaches 1–5, and only slight negative bias at low water temperature for reaches 6–9 (figs. 9 and 10). Therefore, we used the wind function with seasonal evaporation coefficients for all subsequent water temperature predictions (table 7).

Overall, RBM10 performed well in predicting water temperatures of the Klamath River. Predicted water temperature tracked observed temperature closely, capturing both seasonal and shorter term fluctuations in observed water temperatures (figs. 9–11). Consequently, precision for each model reach was favorable. The root mean square error ranged from 0.81 to 1.46°C and mean absolute error ranged from 0.62 to 1.15°C among locations (table 7, figs. 12–13).

Although the calibrated model fit the observed data well, it is important to consider performance when the model is used in predictive mode, outside the range of data used to calibrate the model. Our cross-validation analysis indicated that the model performed well when compared against observed data excluded from the calibration process (table 6, figs. 15 and 16). Aggregate estimates of prediction error from the cross-validation tended to be slightly larger (table 6) when compared to goodness-of-fit statistics from the calibration (table 6), but well within reason for predictive purposes. Had the parameter estimates depended strongly on a particular year of observed data, the prediction error may have been considerably larger than indicated by the calibration statistics. We attribute the favorable prediction error to the extensive set of observed water temperature data used to inform the model. With such a dataset, excluding any given year from the calibration has minor effect on the parameter estimates (table A3).

On average across the 49-year historical time series, the mean of daily-mean water temperature ranged from about 2°C in January to 23°C in July at Iron Gate Dam and from 5° to 22°C at the Trinity River (fig. 17). The 2.5th and 97.5th percentiles of daily temperature for the historical time series yields a 3°C interval about the mean at Iron Gate Dam and a 5°C interval at the Trinity River (fig. 17). The complete time series at each of the calibration sites is shown in figures A1–A9.

Table 6. Best-fit parameter estimates of the wind function shown in equation 11 and goodness-of-fit statistics for observed versus predicted water temperatures at nine locations along the Klamath River.

[Statistics defined as follows: n = sample size, NSS = Nash-Sutcliffe statistic, RMSE = root mean square error, ME = mean error (mean of predicted-observed), MAE = mean absolute error]

Model reach	Location (river mile)	$\hat{a}_r$	$\hat{b}_r$	N	NSS	RMSE	ME	MAE
1	231.9	2.44e-09	7.56e-10	2,488	0.980	1.042	-0.093	0.843
2	189.5	4.77e-09	1.26e-13	10,165	0.965	1.197	-0.329	0.989
3	161.1	4.32e-09	6.79e-15	1,825	0.980	0.946	-0.378	0.774
4	128.5	8.72e-09	1.35e-09	8,461	0.957	1.324	-0.110	1.038
5	100.8	1.59e-09	4.51e-10	1,653	0.971	1.176	-0.094	0.964
6	59.1	4.68e-09	6.34e-11	7,168	0.935	1.608	-0.487	1.260
7	43.7	5.14e-10	2.36e-09	2,283	0.941	1.495	-0.301	1.153
8	16.5	6.94e-15	1.65e-13	1,359	0.963	1.176	-0.254	0.948
9	5.7	1.59e-09	3.44e-11	6,883	0.926	1.543	-0.532	1.227

Table 7. Best-fit parameter estimates of the wind function shown in equation 12 and goodness-of-fit statistics for observed versus predicted water temperatures at nine locations along the Klamath River.

[Statistics defined as follows: n = sample size, NSS = Nash-Sutcliffe statistic, RMSE = root mean square error, ME = mean error (mean of predicted-observed), MAE = mean absolute error]

Model reach	Location (river mile)	$\hat{a}_{r,1}$	$\hat{b}_{r,1}$	$\hat{a}_{r,2}$	$\hat{b}_{r,2}$	n	NSS	RMSE	ME	MAE
1	231.9	2.69e-09	6.39e-10	1.77e-09	8.33e-10	2,488	0.980	1.035	-0.053	0.832
2	189.5	5.11e-09	1.76e-13	2.29e-09	1.36e-13	10,165	0.974	1.029	-0.134	0.804
3	161.1	4.09e-09	2.76e-15	3.24e-09	4.30e-15	1,825	0.985	0.817	-0.183	0.623
4	128.5	8.98e-09	1.75e-09	2.68e-09	4.83e-10	8,461	0.961	1.251	0.072	0.955
5	100.8	1.15e-09	6.76e-10	1.60e-09	2.55e-10	1,653	0.976	1.061	0.095	0.844
6	59.1	4.18e-09	2.28e-10	7.52e-12	2.07e-11	7,168	0.945	1.487	-0.301	1.130
7	43.7	1.21e-09	2.07e-09	1.25e-10	2.25e-09	2,283	0.948	1.403	-0.208	1.052
8	16.5	1.66e-15	1.90e-13	2.89e-15	7.81e-13	1,359	0.965	1.143	-0.199	0.907
9	5.7	1.93e-09	2.53e-11	9.79e-13	3.56e-11	6,883	0.933	1.461	-0.463	1.148

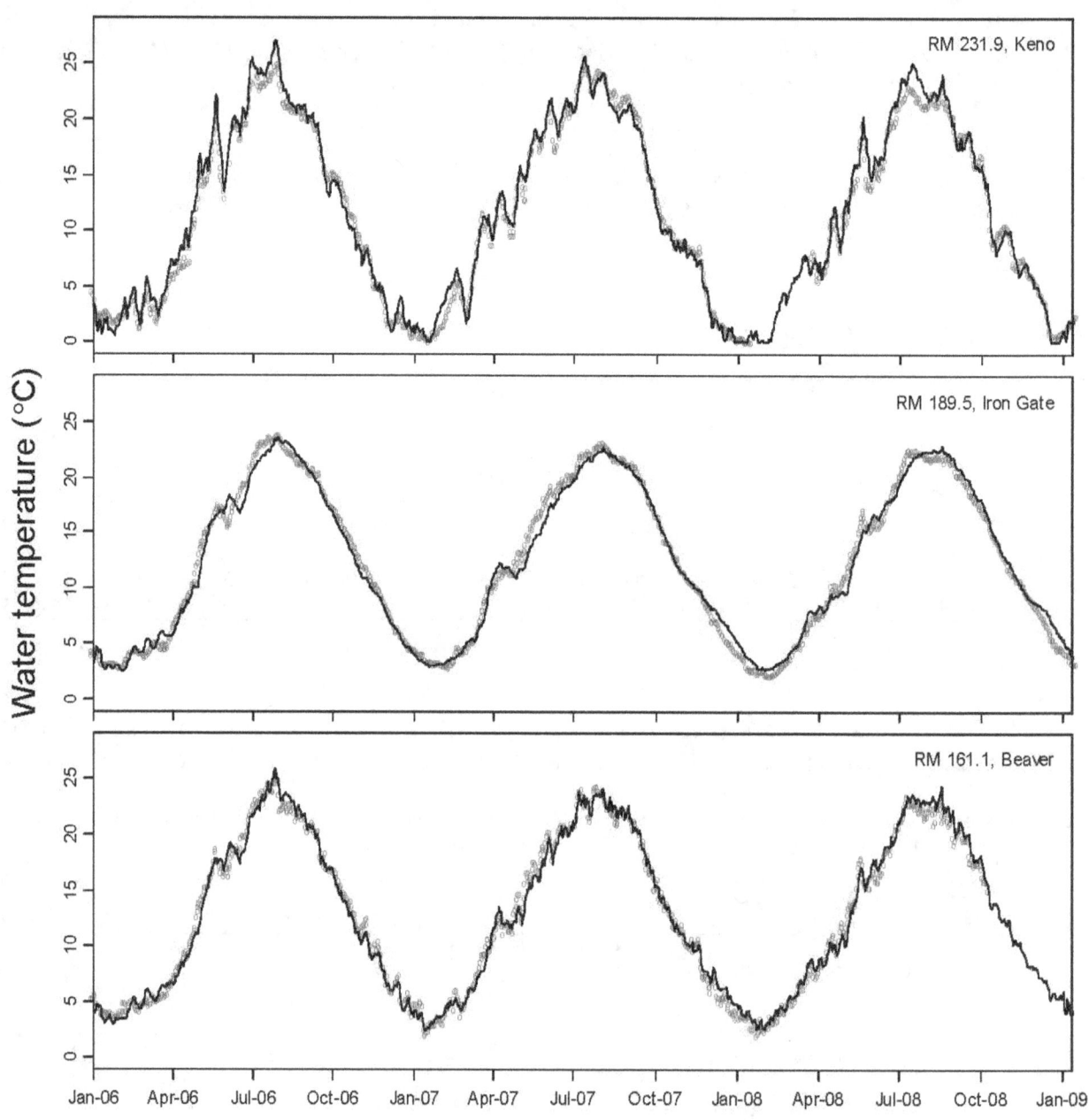

Figure 9.   Time series of predicted (solid line) and observed water temperature (o) of the Klamath River at river miles 231.9, 189.5, and 161.1 for 2006–2009. Water temperature was predicted using the best-fit coefficients from model calibration. The complete 49-year time series is shown in figures A1–A3.

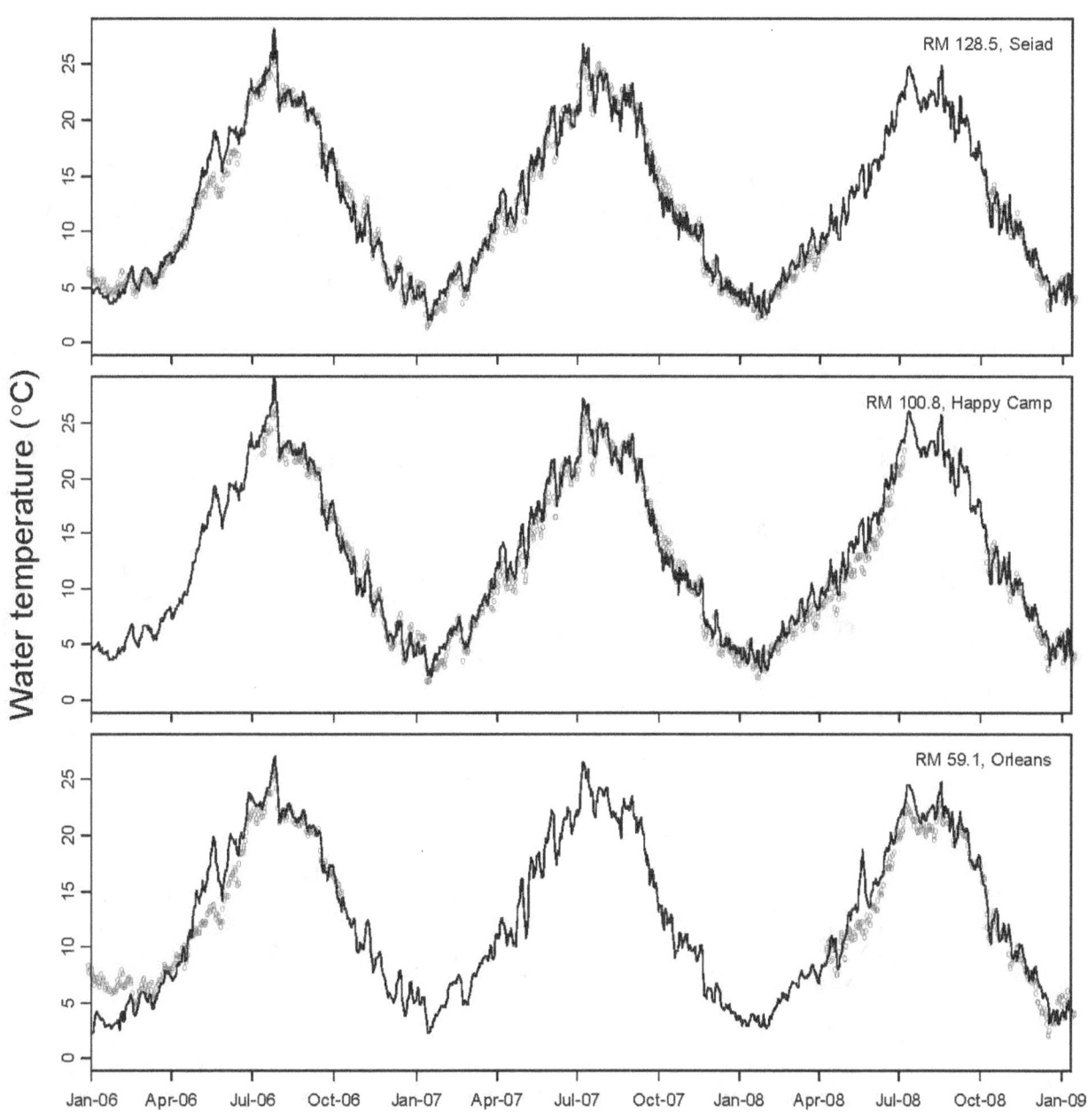

Figure 10. Time series of predicted (solid line) and observed water temperature (o) of the Klamath River at river miles 128.5, 100.8, and 59.1 on the Klamath River for 2006–2009. Water temperature was predicted using the best-fit coefficients from model calibration. The complete 49-year time series is shown in figures A4–A6.

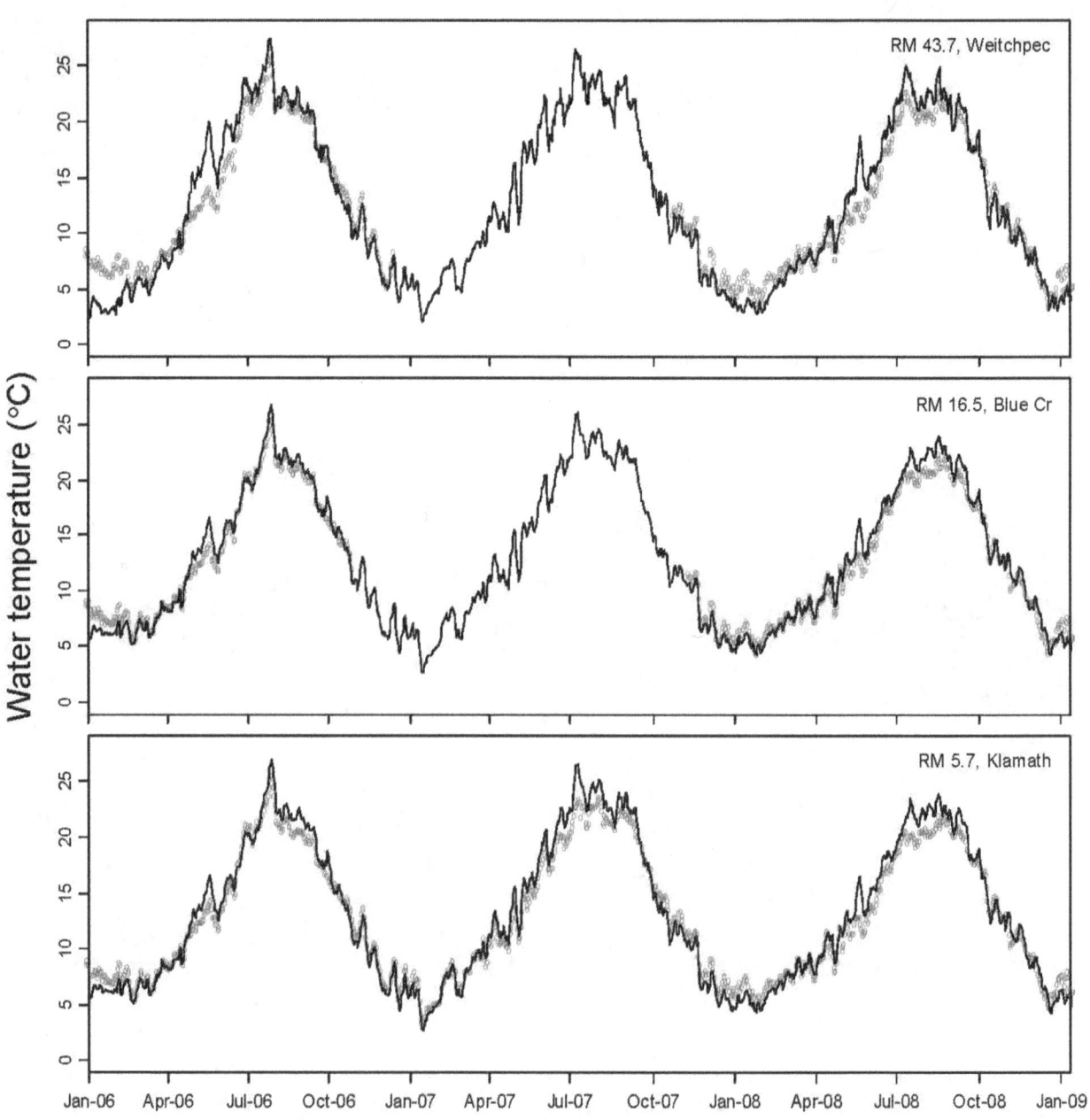

Figure 11. Time series of predicted (solid line) and observed water temperature (o) of the Klamath River at river miles 43.7, 16.5, and 5.7 on the Klamath River for 2006–2009. Water temperature was predicted using the best-fit coefficients from model calibration. The complete 49-year time series is shown in figures A7–A9.

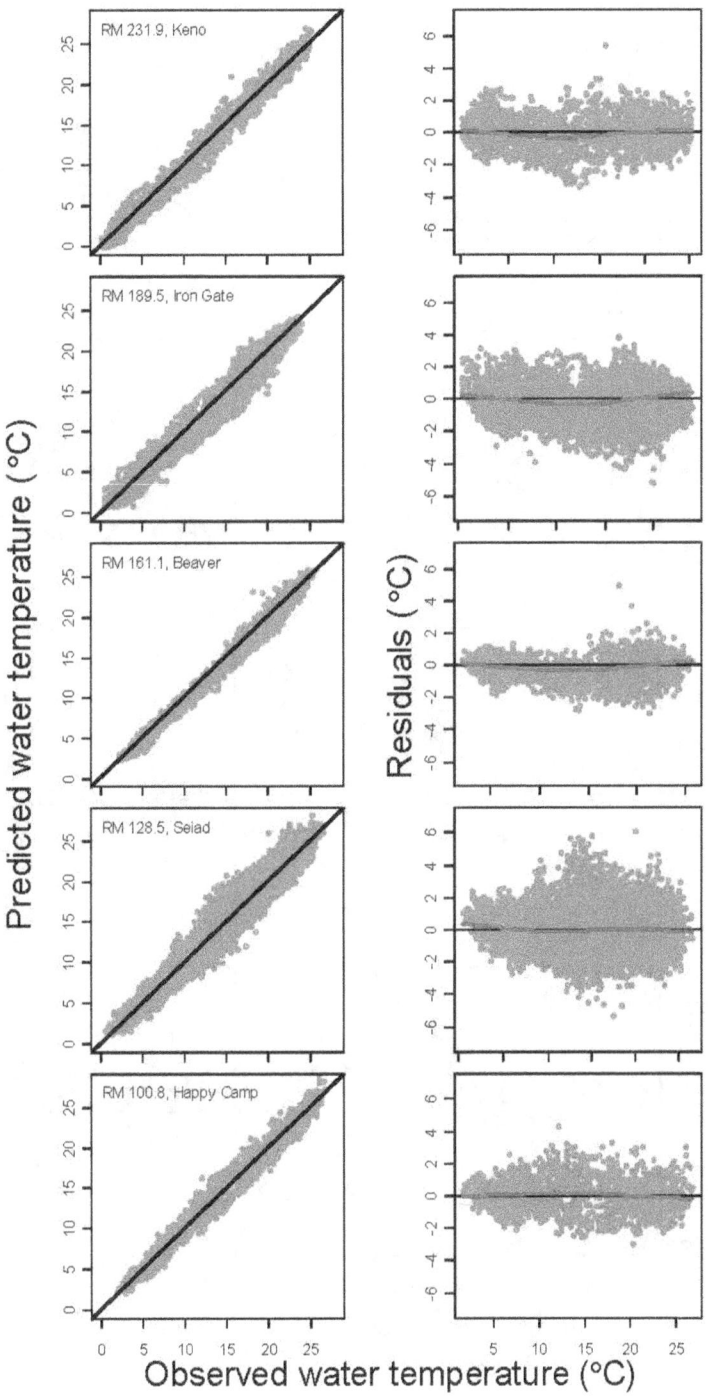

Figure 12. Predicted water temperature and residuals (predicted minus observed temperature) as a function of observed water temperature at five locations between river miles (RM) 231.9 and 100.8 of the Klamath River. The red line shows a LOWESS smoother (locally weighted polynomial regression) to illustrate the trend in the residuals.

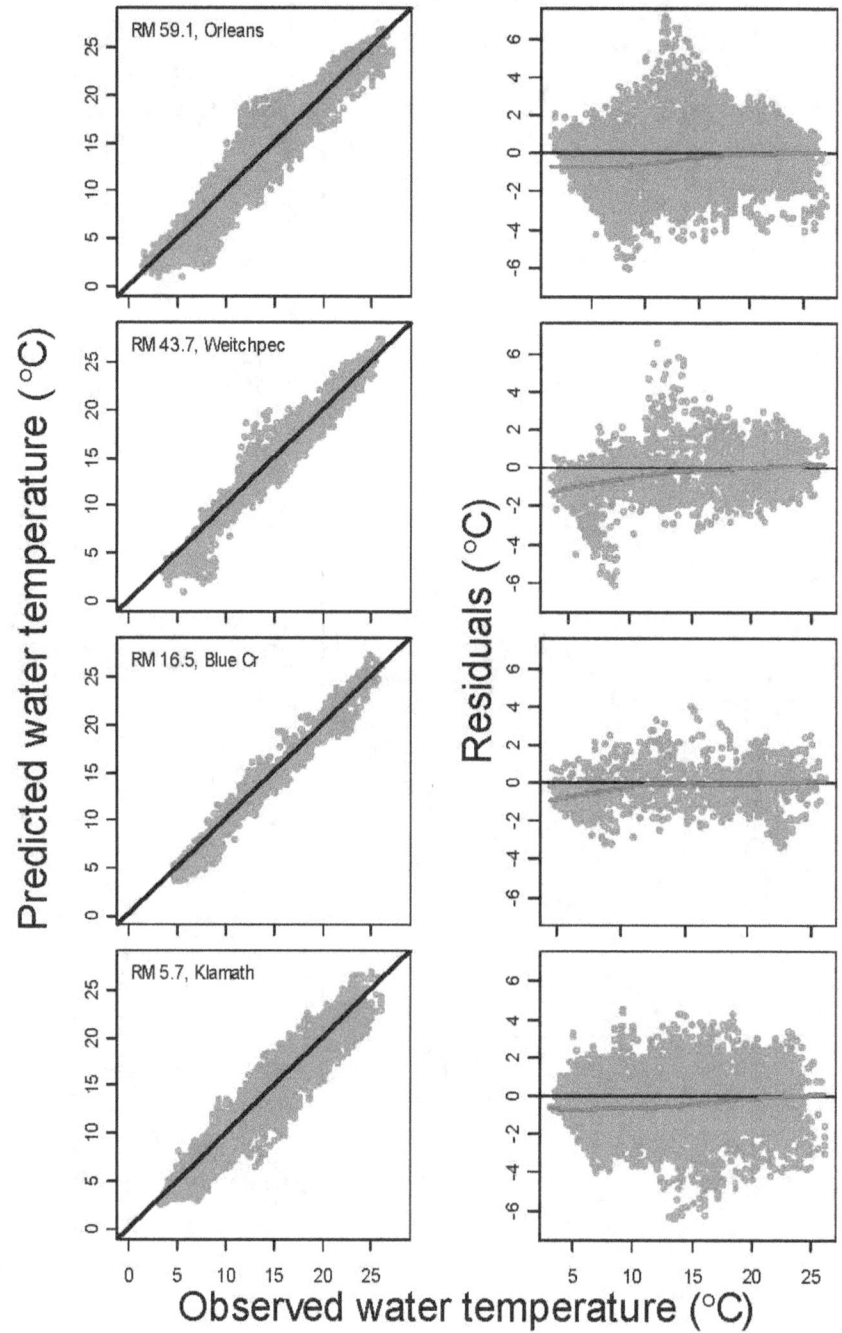

Figure 13. Predicted water temperature and residuals (predicted minus observed temperature) as a function of observed water temperature at five locations between river miles (RM) 59.1 and 5.7 of the Klamath River. The red line shows a LOWESS smoother (locally weighted polynomial regression) to illustrate the trend in the residuals.

Table 8. Aggregate cross-validation estimates of prediction error for evaluating observed versus predicted water temperatures at nine locations along the Klamath River.

[The aggregate cross-validation estimates are the weighted averages of the yearly estimates shown in table A3. Statistics defined as follows: NSS = Nash-Sutcliffe statistic, RMSE = root mean square error, ME = mean error, MAE = mean absolute error]

Reach	River mile	Number of years	NSS	RMSE	ME	MAE
1	231.9	10	0.976	1.058	-0.072	0.863
2	189.5	33	0.967	1.020	-0.134	0.808
3	161.1	8	0.960	0.815	-0.183	0.634
4	128.5	29	0.952	1.232	0.087	0.963
5	100.8	8	0.933	1.067	0.105	0.856
6	59.1	25	0.937	1.425	-0.304	1.135
7	43.7	11	0.921	1.334	-0.191	1.059
8	16.5	7	0.910	1.106	-0.199	0.907
9	5.7	25	0.908	1.411	-0.459	1.156

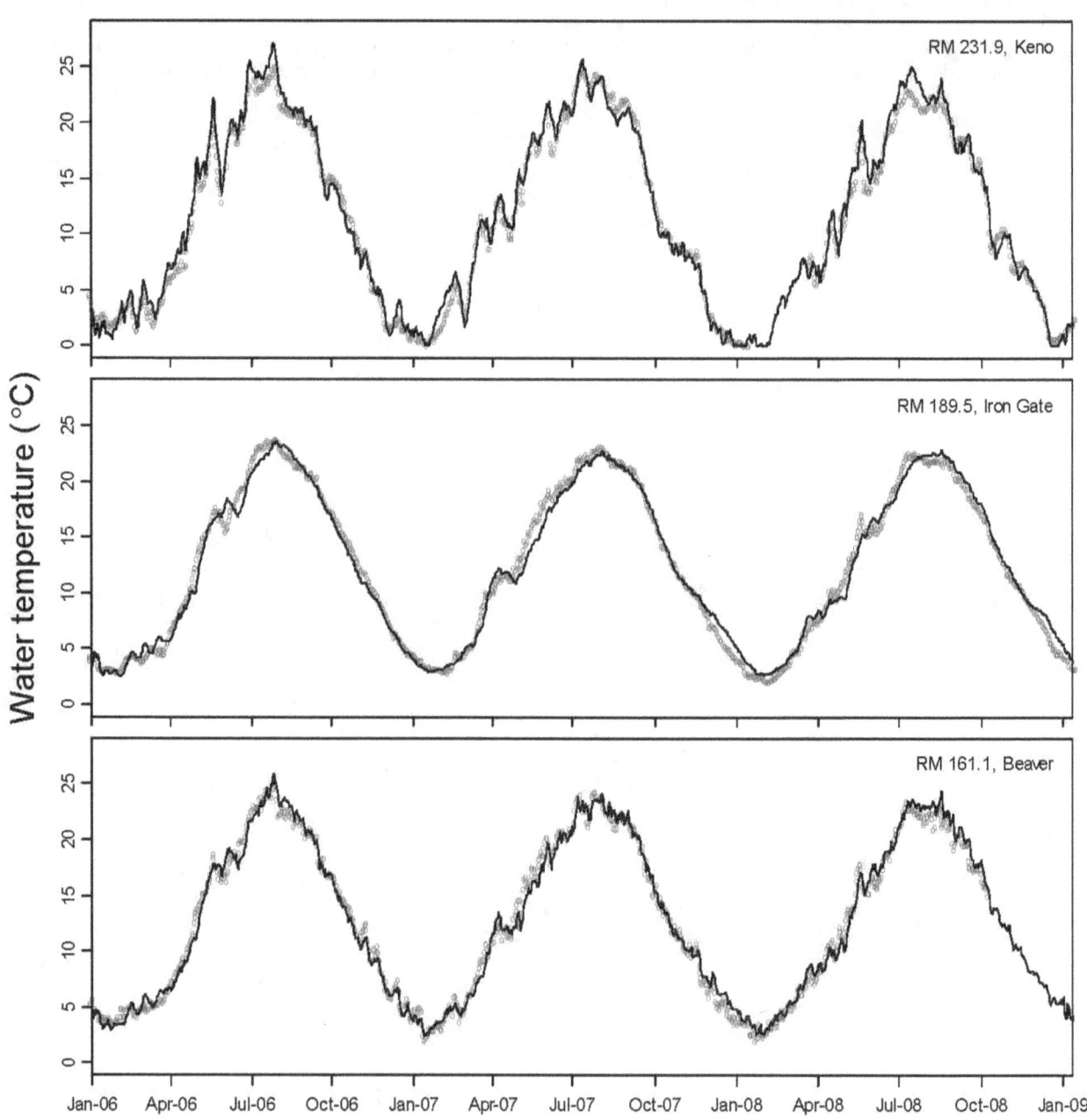

Figure 14. Validation plots showing time series of predicted (solid line) and observed water temperature (o) of the Klamath River at river miles 231.9, 189.5, and 161.1 on the Klamath River for 2006–2009. For each year *k*, water temperature was predicted by estimating model coefficients with *k*th year of observed data excluded, and then using those coefficients to predict water temperature in year *k* (see table A3).

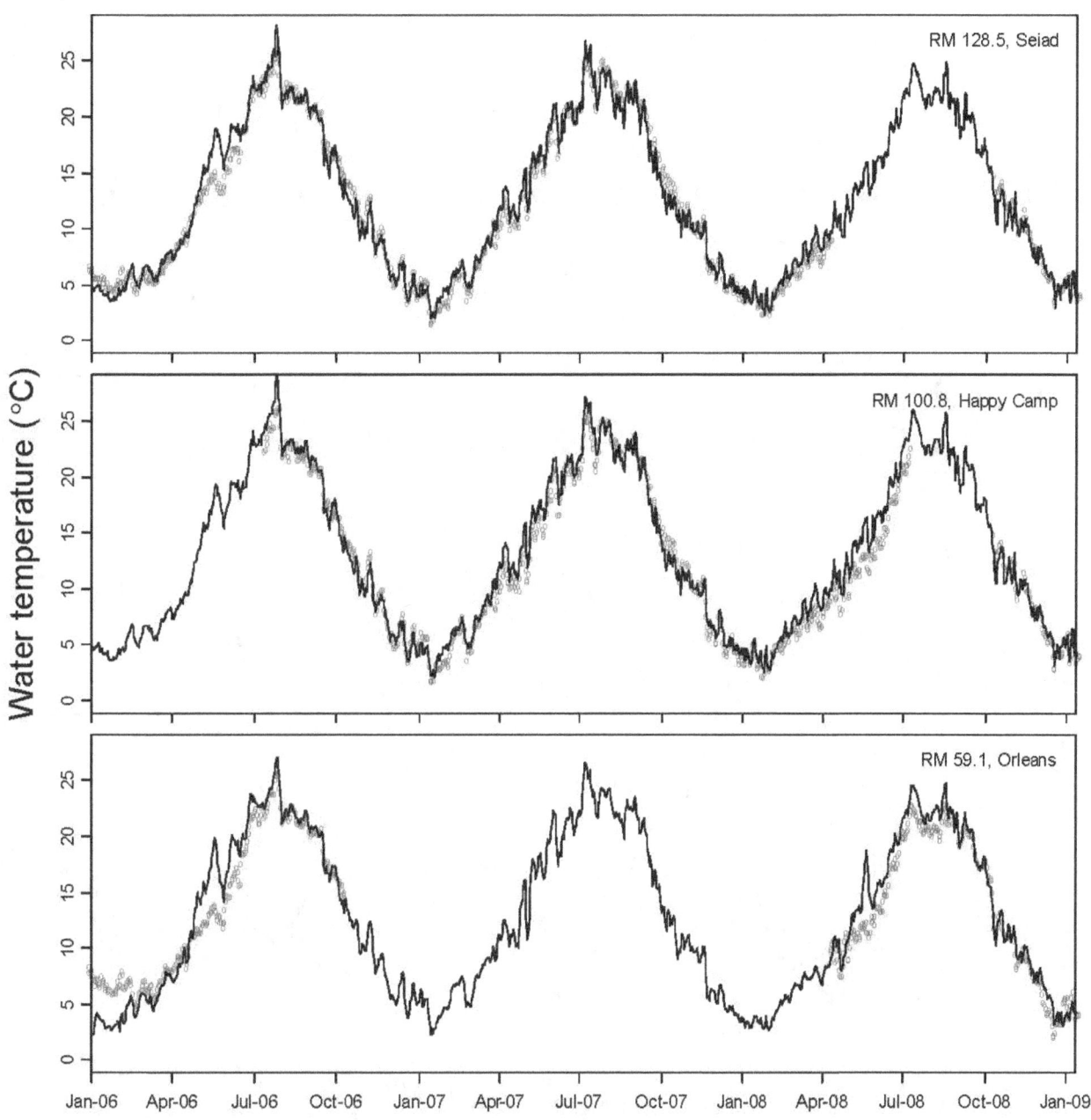

Figure 15. Validation plots showing time series of predicted (solid line) and observed water temperature (o) of the Klamath River at river miles 128.5, 100.8, and 59.1 on the Klamath River for 2006–2009. For each year *k*, water temperature was predicted by estimating model coefficients with *k*th year of observed data excluded, and then using those coefficients to predict water temperature in year *k* (see table A3).

31

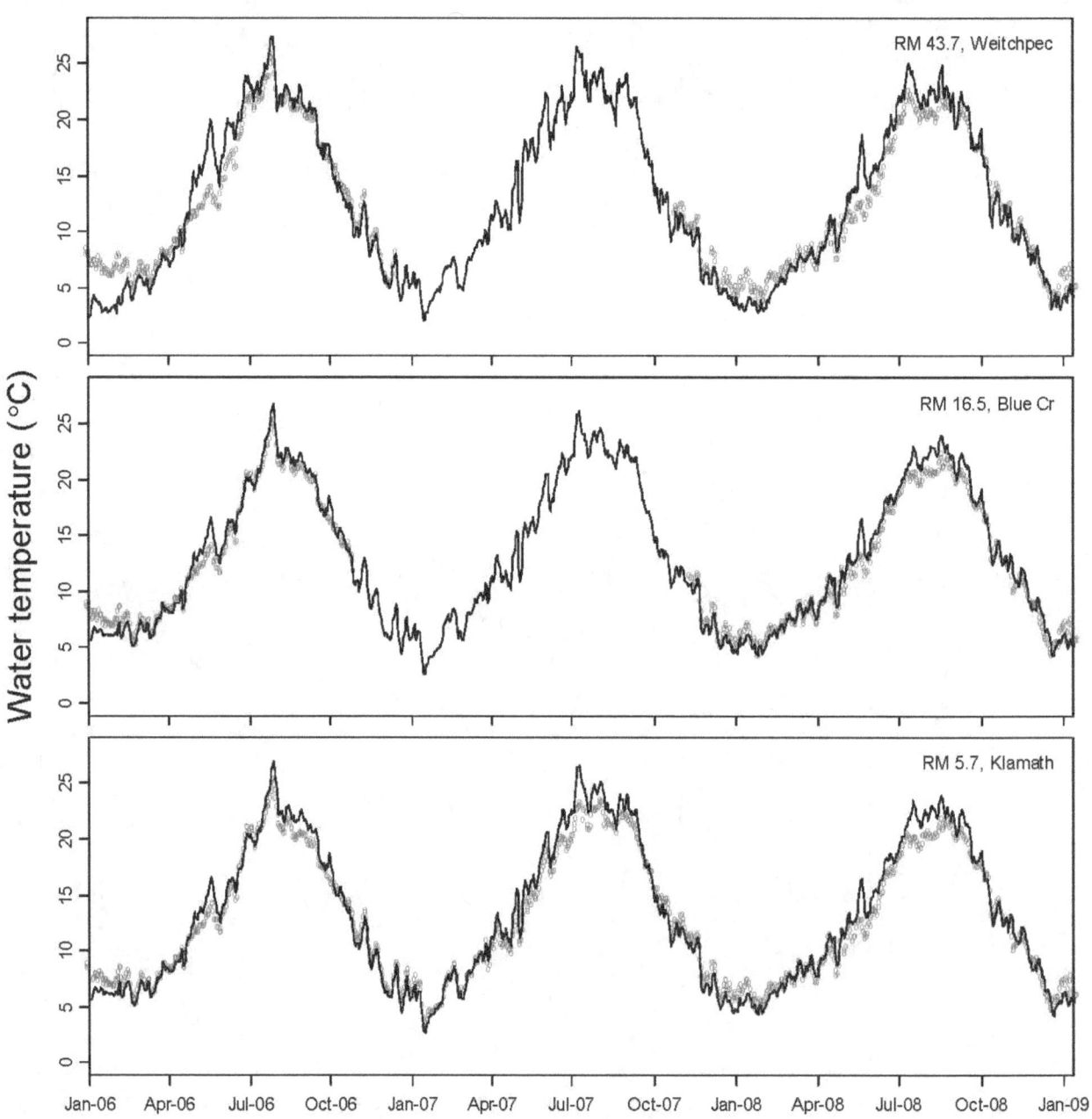

Figure 16. Validation plots showing time series of predicted (solid line) and observed water temperature (o) of the Klamath River at river miles 43.7, 16.5, and 5.7 on the Klamath River for 2006–2009. For each year *k*, water temperature was predicted by estimating model coefficients with *k*th year of observed data excluded, and then using those coefficients to predict water temperature in year *k* (see table A3).

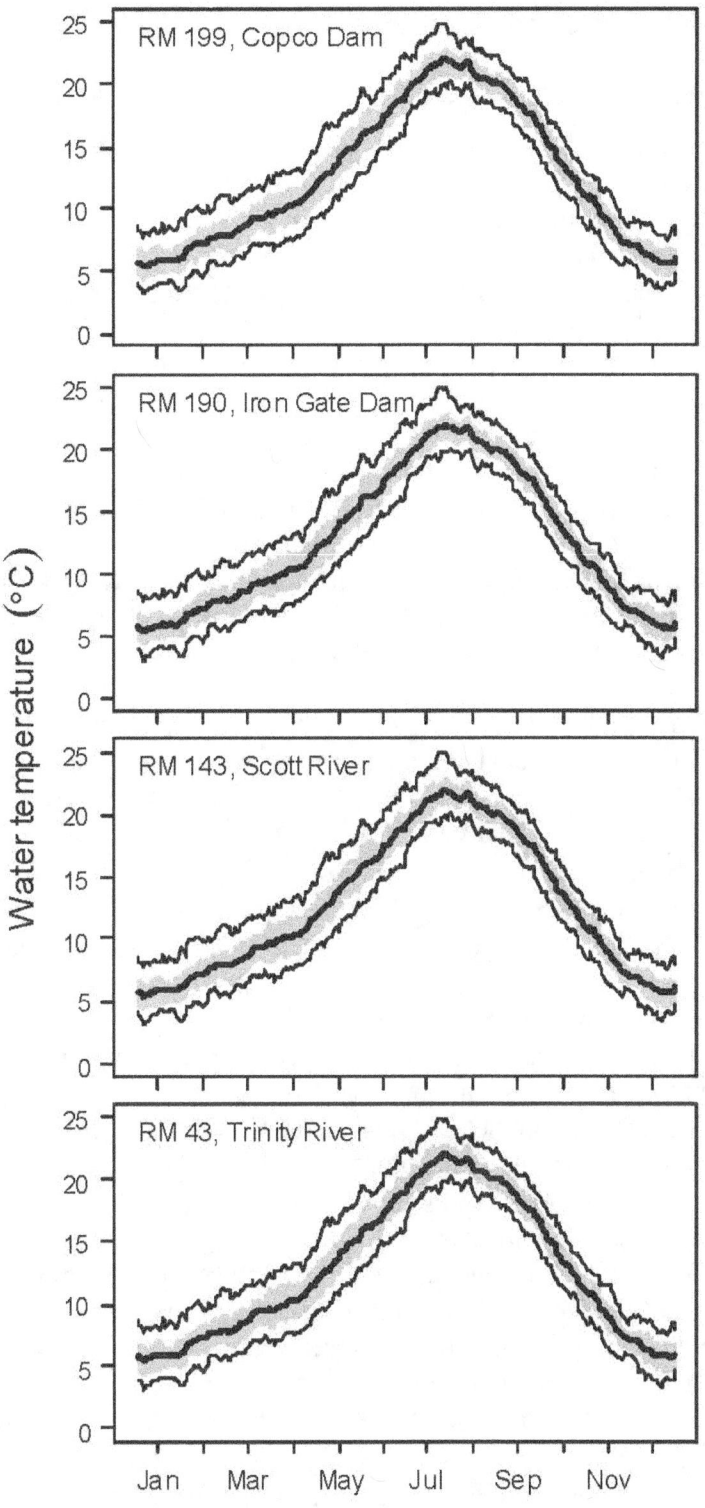

Figure 17. Summary of the 49-year historical time series of daily mean water temperatures at four locations on the Klamath River. The heavy line shows the mean temperature on a given day, the shaded area shows the interquartile range (25th–75th percentiles), and the thin lines bound the 2.5th–97.5th percentiles.

Management Alternatives and Climate Scenarios

Comparing Biological Opinion and Klamath Basin Restoration Agreement under Historical Climate

We focused on the Index Sequential climate scenario to evaluate the effects of BO and KBRA alternatives on water temperature in the absence of climate change. Differences in mean daily water temperature between BO and KBRA depended on location and time period (that is, before or after dam removal). Prior to dam removal (before 2020), we found very little difference in daily mean water temperatures between BO and KBRA (figs. 18–20). After dam removal, differences in daily water temperatures depend on location. The largest differences between BO and KBRA occurs at Iron Gate Dam after dam removal (fig. 18), but temperature differences diminish at points downstream of Iron Gate Dam as major tributaries contribute to the Klamath River (figs. 18–20). At Iron Gate Dam, daily fluctuation in water temperature increases considerably after dam removal (fig. 18). Furthermore, the temperature cycle shifts after dam removal, with water temperatures rising earlier and descending earlier in the year. Downstream of the Scott River, we found little difference in daily mean water temperatures between BO and KBRA alternatives following dam removal (figs. 19 and 20).

Annual-mean water temperatures reveal whether BO or KBRA increase or decrease water temperature, on average, relative to the historical time series. Similar to the daily time series, we found little difference among historical, BO, and KBRA prior to 2020 (fig. 21). After 2020, when dams are removed under KBRA, annual-mean water temperatures were consistently lower than historically at Copco and Iron Gate Dams, but varied little from the historical temperatures downstream of the Scott River (fig. 21). In contrast, annual-mean temperatures of BO were consistently higher than the historical time series (fig. 21) at Iron Gate Dam, but not elsewhere. Although we found systematic differences of each management alternative relative to historical temperatures, the magnitudes of the difference are relatively small. At Iron Gate Dam, the maximum difference from the historical was about 0.5°C under BO and about -1.0°C under KBRA (fig. 22). On average, annual-mean temperatures after 2020 at Iron Gate Dam were 0.46°C less than historical under KBRA and 0.31°C greater than historical under BO (fig. 22).

Simulated mean water temperatures by Julian day revealed a similar trend to the daily time series suggesting a general pattern across the 50-year simulation period. Prior to dam removal (2012–2019), mean temperatures by Julian day are nearly identical between BO and KBRA alternatives, and neither alternative differs from the historical simulation (fig. 23). Following dam removal under KBRA, we observed a shift to an earlier temperature cycle and a slightly lower maximum temperature, on average, at Copco and Iron Gate Dams (≤1°C; fig. 23). Under the BO alternative, the temperature cycle for 2020–2061 was nearly identical to the historical temperature cycle. From Scott River downstream, we observed little difference in the mean temperature cycle after dam removal (fig. 23).

In the vicinity of the dams, the shift in the water temperature cycle is projected to increase river temperatures in the spring, result in little difference in summer, and decrease temperatures in the fall (figs. 18 and 24). For example, mean temperature in May is projected to increase by about 2°C after dam removal near Iron Gate Dam, and by about 1°C at the Scott River (fig. 24). Mean temperature differences in May continue to diminish moving downstream of Scott River to the ocean (fig. 24). In July, when the peak of the temperature cycle typically is observed (fig. 23), we found mean temperature differences of less than or equal to 1°C across the longitudinal profile of the Klamath River. The largest projected differences in mean temperature occur in the fall (fig. 23). For example, in October, simulated mean temperatures decreased by 4°C at Iron Gate Dam, by about 2°C near the Scott River, and by less than 1°C at the Trinity River (fig. 23). In late summer (September), warm water temperature conditions

34

combined with low streamflows, can be of particular concern to fish health due to potential disease outbreaks. The 2002 salmon die-off in the lower Klamath River occurred at that time of year. Figure 23 shows that dam removal would decrease temperatures by several degrees at locations near Copco and Iron Gate Dams. However, the change in temperatures would be less noticeable at locations farther downstream.

Seasonal water temperature differences are caused more by a shift in the temperature cycle than a change in mean annual temperature. To quantify the temporal shift in the temperature cycle, we estimated the phase shift by fitting a sin function of the form:

$$T = A\left(\frac{2\pi}{365.25}d + \theta\right) + D$$
                                                                                                  (13)

where T is the mean water temperature on Julian day d, A is the amplitude, θ is the phase, and D is the mean annual temperature. The phase shift was then estimated as

$$\frac{365.25}{2\pi}\left(\hat{\theta}_{BO} - \hat{\theta}_{KBRA}\right).$$

Following dam removal, we found that temperature cycle shifts, on average, by about 18 days earlier at Iron Gate Dam; by about 6 days earlier at the Scott River, and by about 2 days at the Trinity River (fig. 25). Furthermore, we found the same trend in phase shift for all climate scenarios (fig. 25).

Influence of Climate Change on Water Temperature

Annual mean water temperatures for all GCMs increased over the 2012–2061 simulation period under both BO and KBRA alternatives (figs. 26 and 27). However, between Copco and Iron Gate Dams, dam removal under KBRA mediated and delayed the effects of climate change to some extent (fig. 27), relative to BO where dams remain in place (fig. 26). For example, at Iron Gate Dam, annual-mean temperatures under BO exceed the 49-year historical mean beginning in 2025 (fig. 26). In contrast, under KBRA, annual mean temperatures consistently exceed the historical mean temperature beginning in 2045 (fig. 27). By the end of the 50-year time series, annual mean water temperature under KBRA were about 1°C less than under BO at Iron Gate Dam. Downstream of the Scott River, we observed little difference in the annual mean temperature between KBRA and BO (figs. 26 and 27).

The decadal mean of simulated water temperatures shows progressive incremental increases with each decade from 2012 to 2061 (fig. 28). Furthermore, nearly all decades show an increase relative to the 49-year historical mean water temperature for all scenarios (fig. 28). Under the climate change scenarios, mean decadal water temperature increases by about 1–2.3°C over the 50-year horizon, depending on GCM (fig. 29). Among GCM models, increases in water temperature generally followed the quantile rankings of air temperature for the GCM models. The MIUB model was "warmest and driest" GCM (75th temperature and 25th precipitation quantile, table 4) and produced the largest projected increase in water temperature (fig. 28). Although the MRI model was the "coolest and wettest" (25th temperature and 75th precipitation quantile, table 4), the "coolest and driest" model (NCAR) produced the lowest projected increase in water temperature over the simulation period.

It is important to recognize that the Index Sequential scenario is based on historical hydrology and meteorology from 1961 to 2009. Thus, each decadal mean shows how water temperature changed from 1961 to 2009 had BO or KBRA been implemented. From this perspective, mean water temperature increased with each passing decade under both BO and KBRA (fig. 28). Under KBRA after dam removal, the increase in temperature relative to the long-term historical mean is a fraction of a degree less than under BO in the reach between Iron Gate Dam and the Scott River (fig. 29, top panels).

Seasonal changes in water temperature under climate change (fig. 30) were similar to the Index Sequential simulation (fig. 23), with the exception that both the BO and KBRA temperatures under climate change typically were higher than the historical temperatures (see also figs. A10–A13). At Copco and Iron Gate Dams during the dams out period, increases in predicted temperature relative to the historical simulation are fairly constant throughout the year (fig. 30). At the Trinity River however, simulated temperatures under climate change were similar to the historical temperatures during fall and winter, but higher during spring and summer (fig. 30). These general patterns were consistent among all GCMs (figs. A10–A13). As mentioned above, the late summer (September) period is of particular concern to fish health. Figure 30 shows that under climate change dam removal would still decrease temperatures at locations near Copco and Iron Gate Dams for this time of the year. However, the decrease in temperatures would be offset by the warming effect of climate change as seen by comparing figure 30 with figure 23.

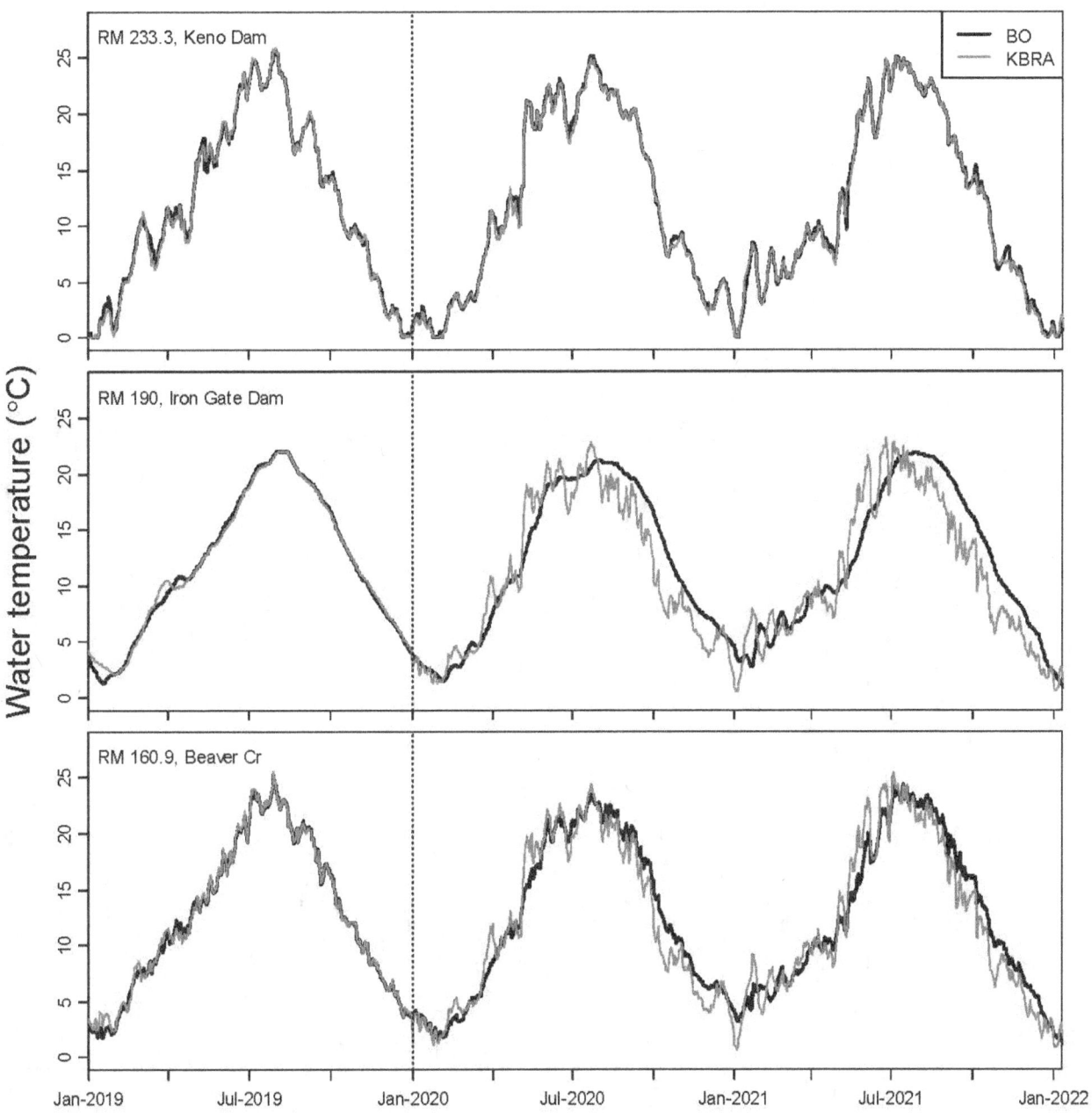

Figure 18. Time series of simulated daily water temperature at river miles 233.3, 190.0, and 160.9 under the Index Sequential climate with KBRA (dams out) and BO (dams in) management scenarios. The 3 years shown include 1 year prior and 2 years following dam removal, with 2019–2021 corresponding to historical hydrology and meteorology of 1968–70. The dashed vertical line indicates when dams were removed in the simulation.

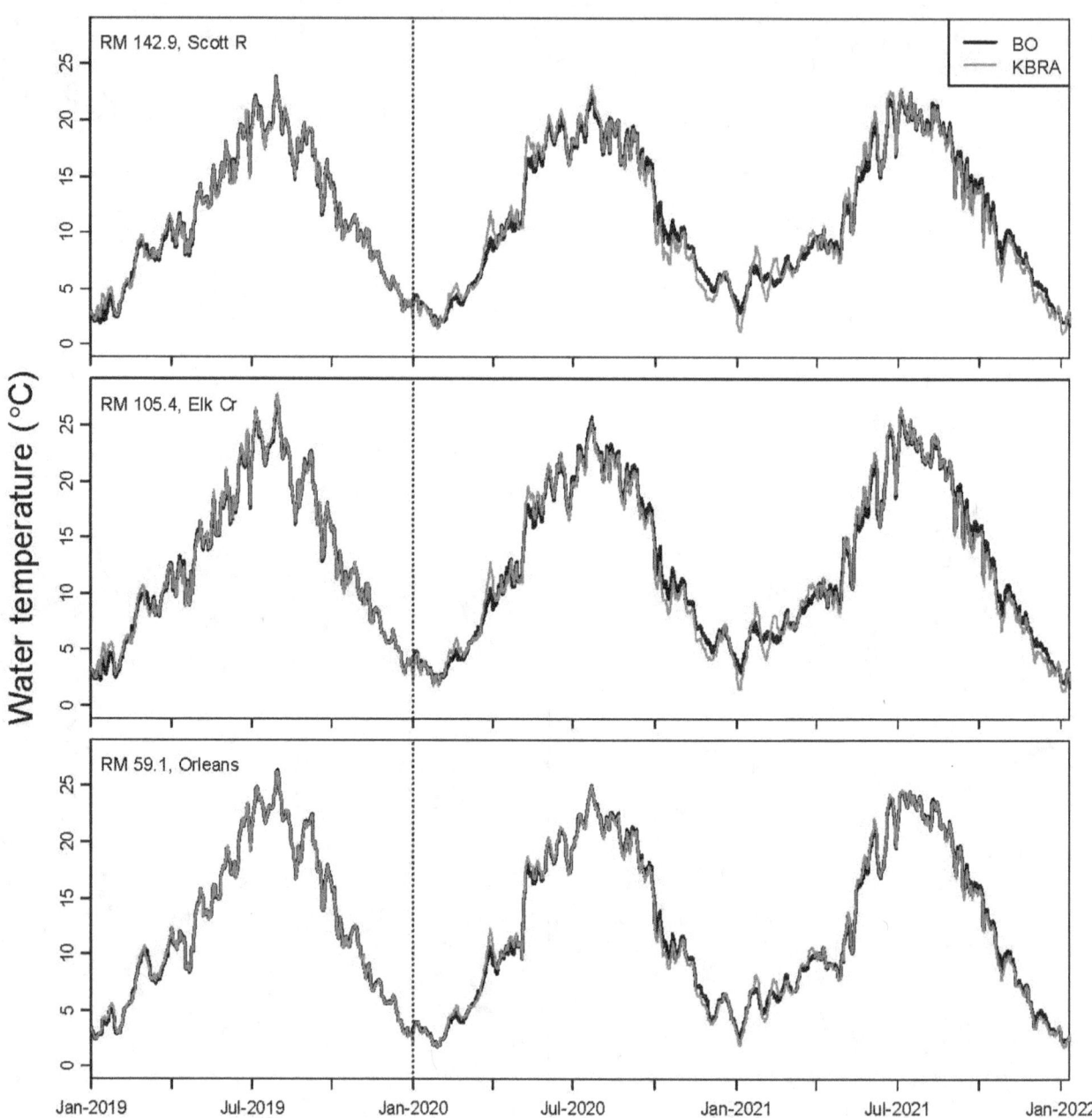

Figure 19. Time series of simulated daily water temperature at river miles 142.9, 105.4, and 59.1 under the Index Sequential climate with KBRA (dams out) and BO (dams in) management scenarios. The 3 years shown include 1 year prior and 2 years following dam removal, with 2019–2021 corresponding to historical hydrology and meteorology of 1968–70. The dashed vertical line indicates when dams were removed in the simulation.

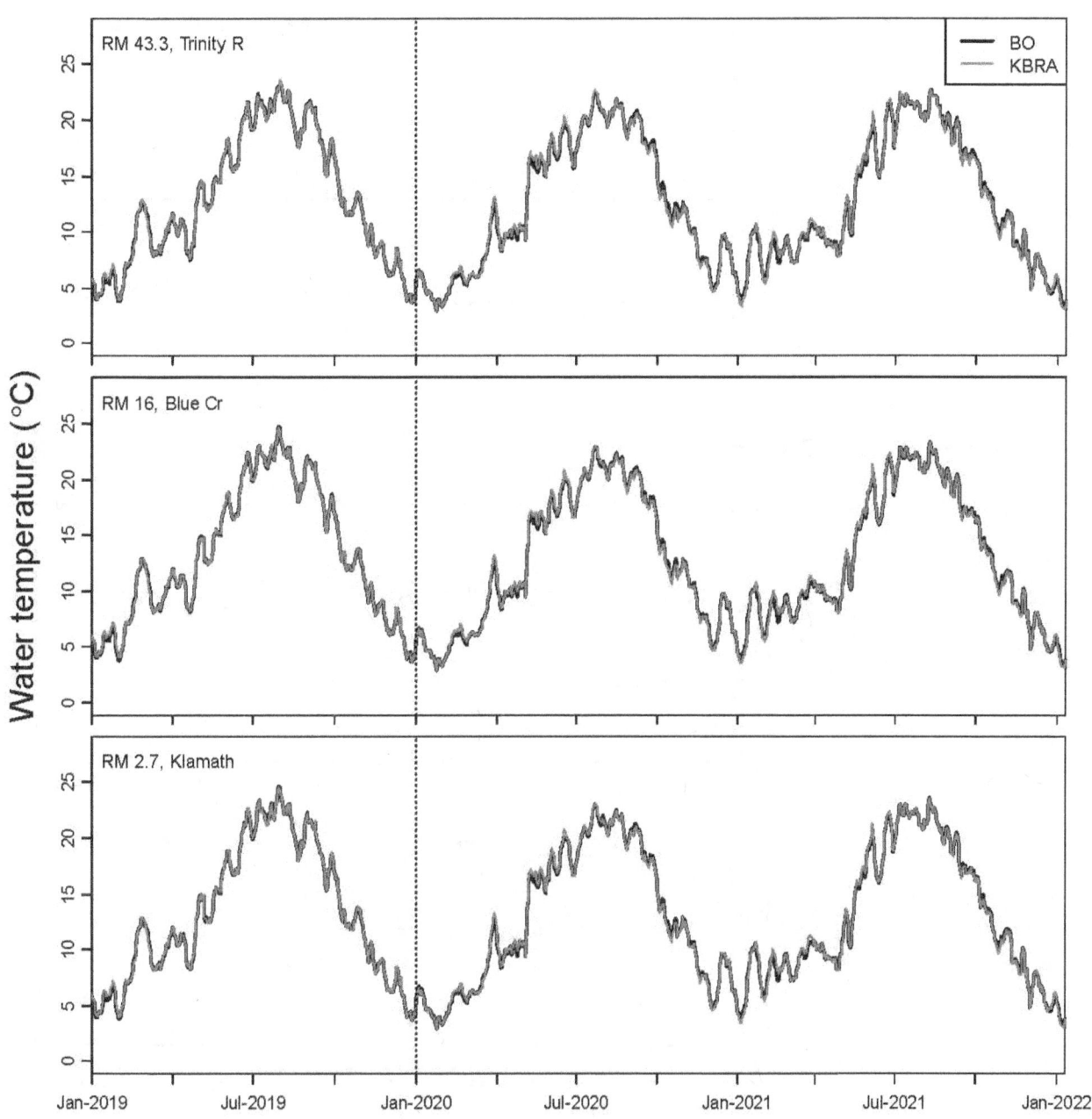

Figure 20. Time series of simulated daily water temperature at river miles 43.3, 16.0, and 2.7 under the Index Sequential climate with KBRA (dams out) and BO (dams in) management scenarios. The 3 years shown include 1 year prior and 2 years following dam removal, with 2019–2021 corresponding to historical hydrology and meteorology of 1968–70. The dashed vertical line indicates when dams were removed in the simulation.

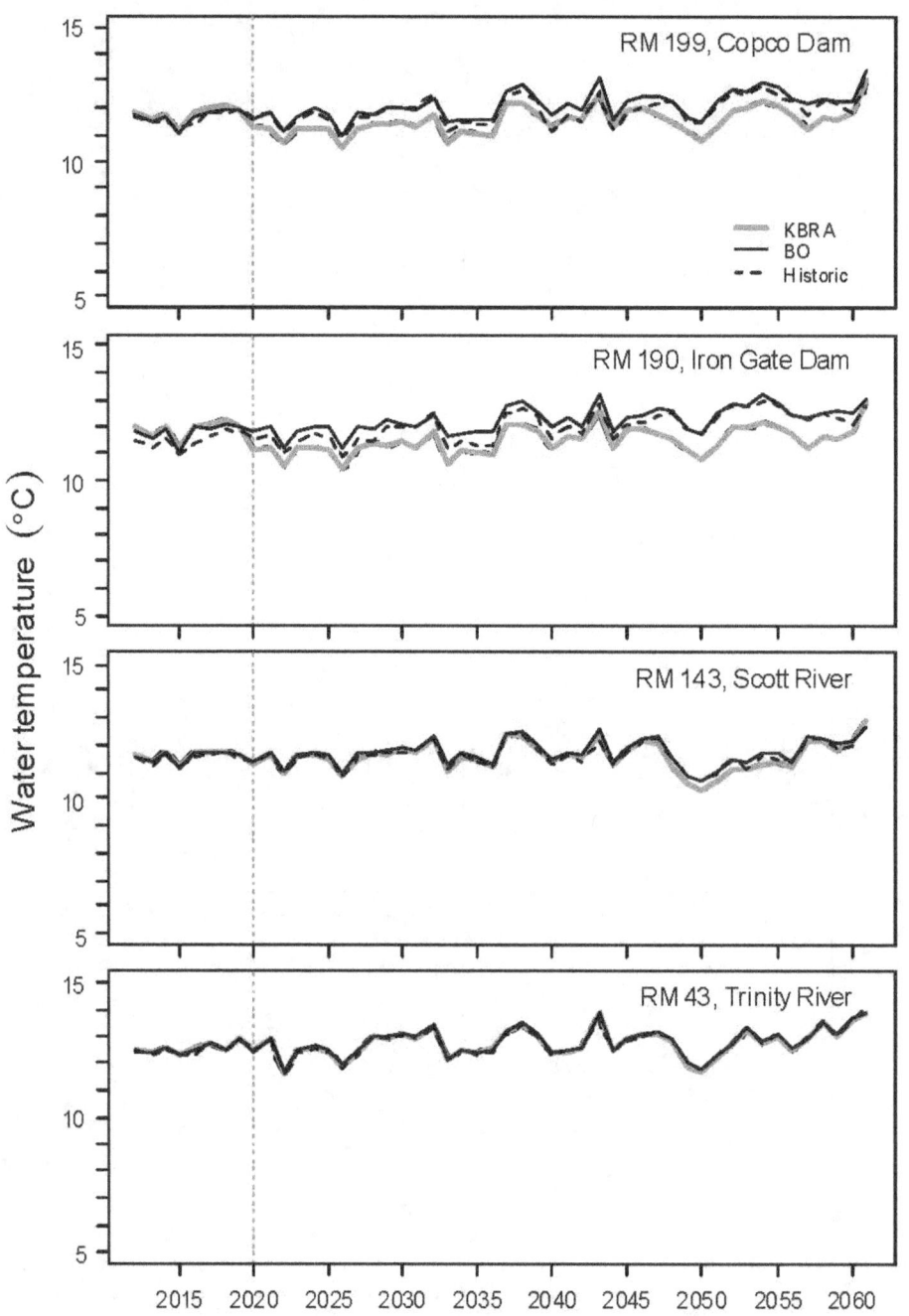

Figure 21. Time series of annual mean water temperature simulated by RBM10 for historical simulation, as well as KBRA and BO under the Index Sequential climate scenario. The historical time series (1961–2009) is plotted for the corresponding years under the Index Sequential scenario (2012–2061) with 1961 repeated for 2061. The vertical reference line shows when dams are removed under the KBRA alternative.

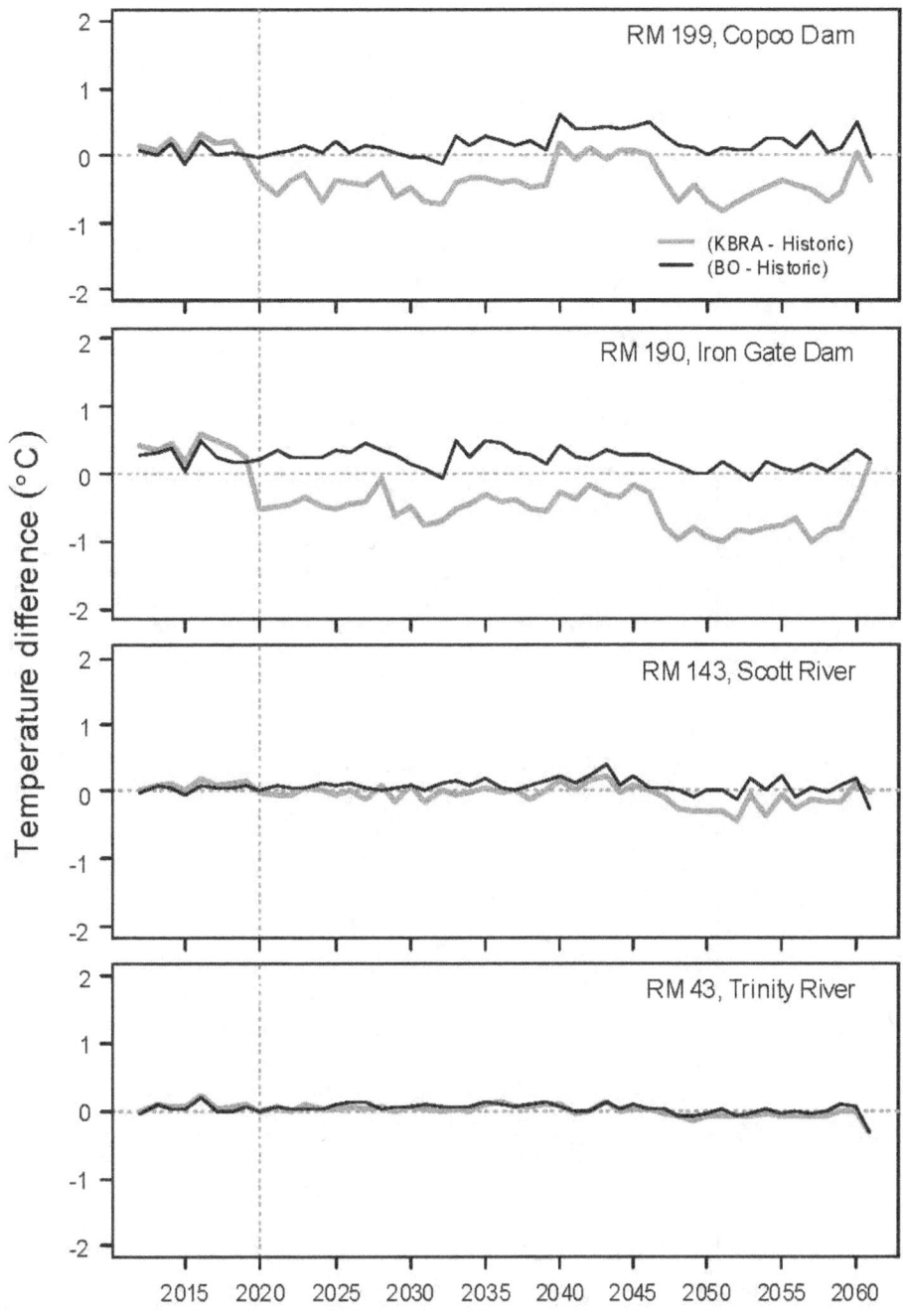

Figure 22. Time series of the difference in simulated historical annual mean water temperatures from KBRA and BO management options under the Index Sequential climate scenario. The vertical reference line shows when dams are removed under the KBRA alternative.

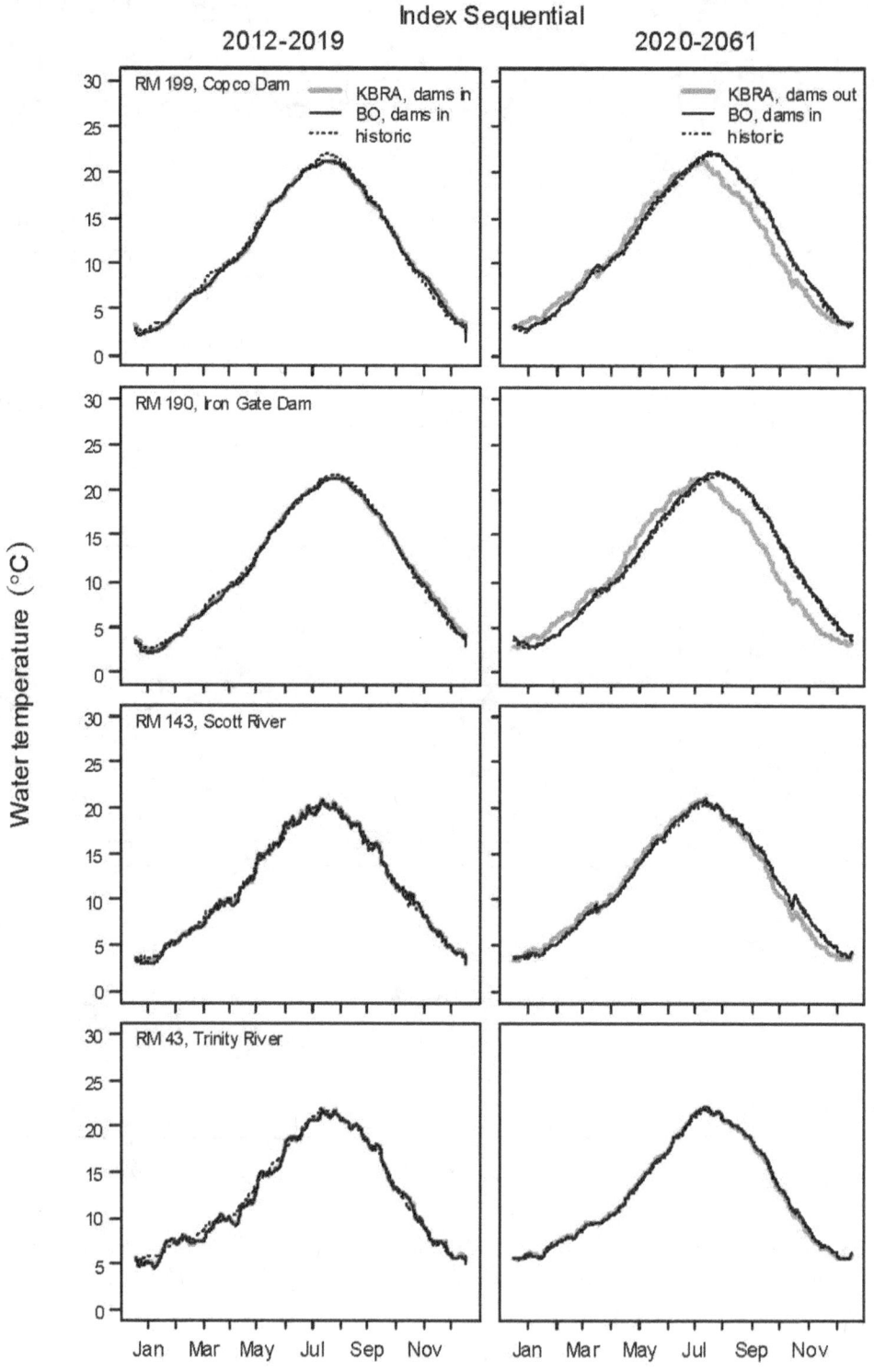

Figure 23. Mean temperature by Julian day for the KBRA dams in period (left panels) and dams out period (right panels) at four locations on the Klamath River for the Index Sequential simulation. The historical simulation is shown as a baseline and represents mean temperatures by Julian day for 1961–2009.

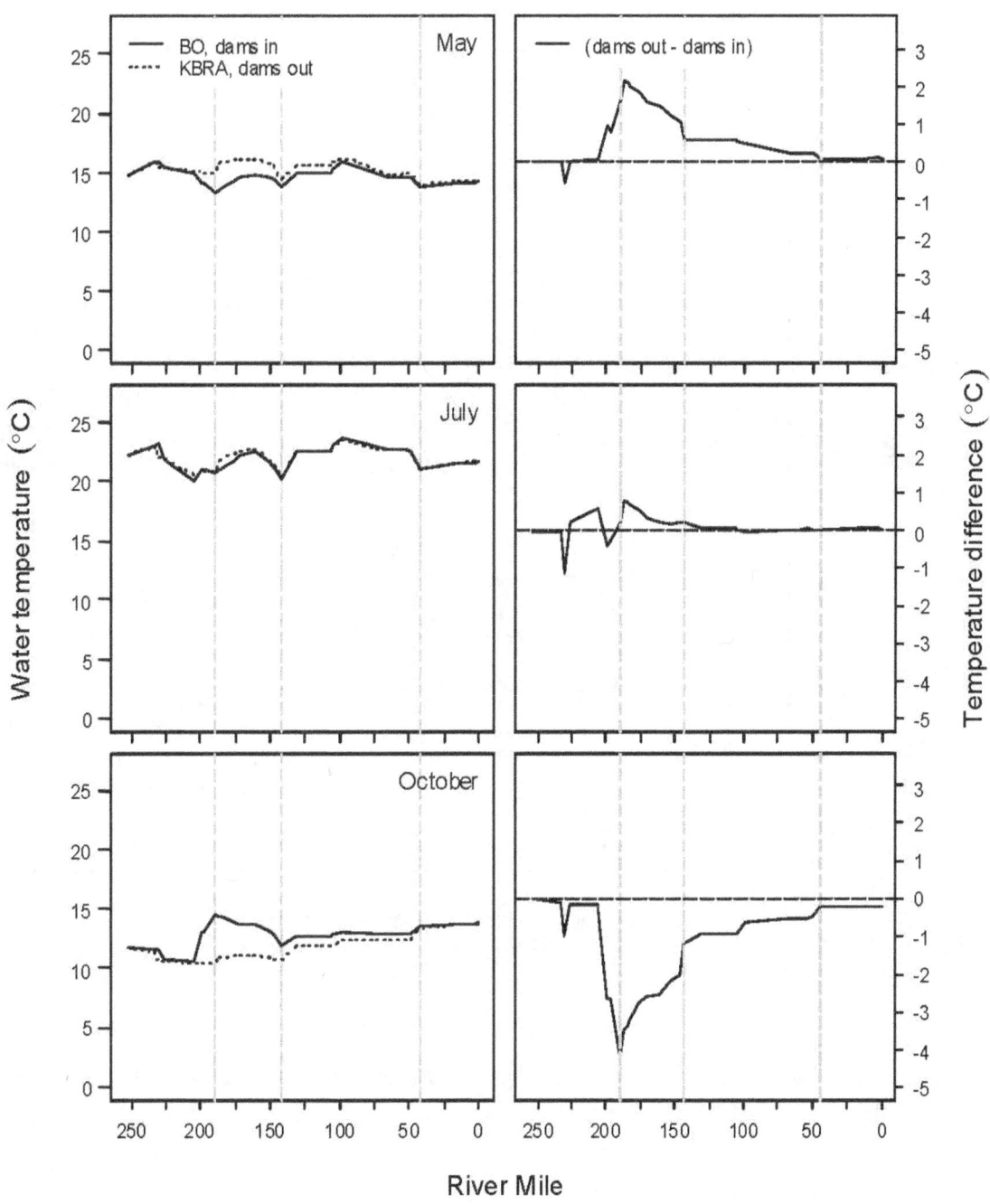

Figure 24. Predicted mean monthly temperature in May, July, and October (left panels) and temperature difference (right panels) between KBRA (dams out) and BO (dams in) scenarios by river mile for the Index Sequential climate scenario for the dams out period (2020–61). Vertical reference lines mark the location of Iron Gate Dam (RM 190, RM = river mile), the Scott River (RM 142.9), and the Trinity River (RM 43.3).

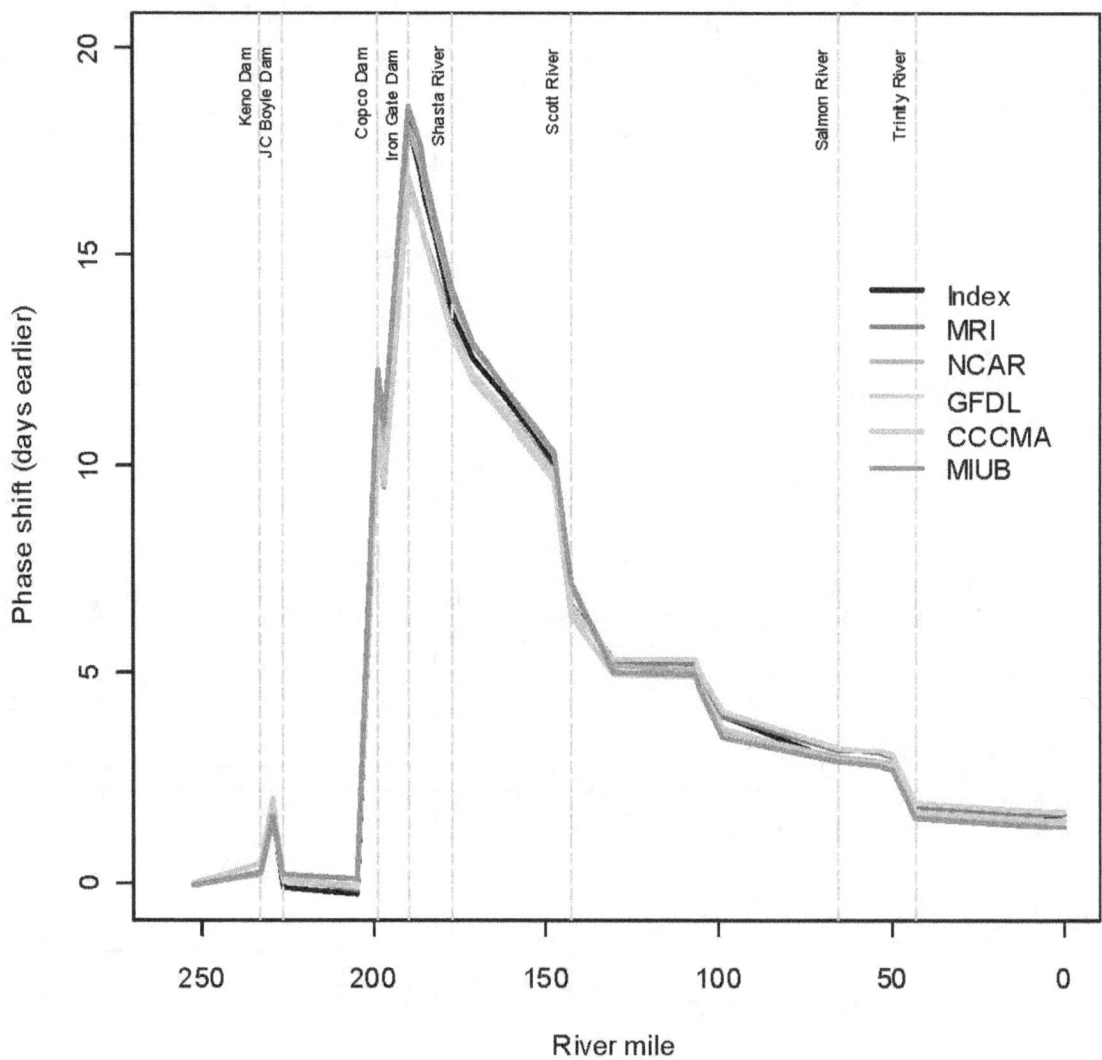

Figure 25. Projected shift in the annual temperature cycle due to dam removal (days earlier after dam removal) as a function of river mile.

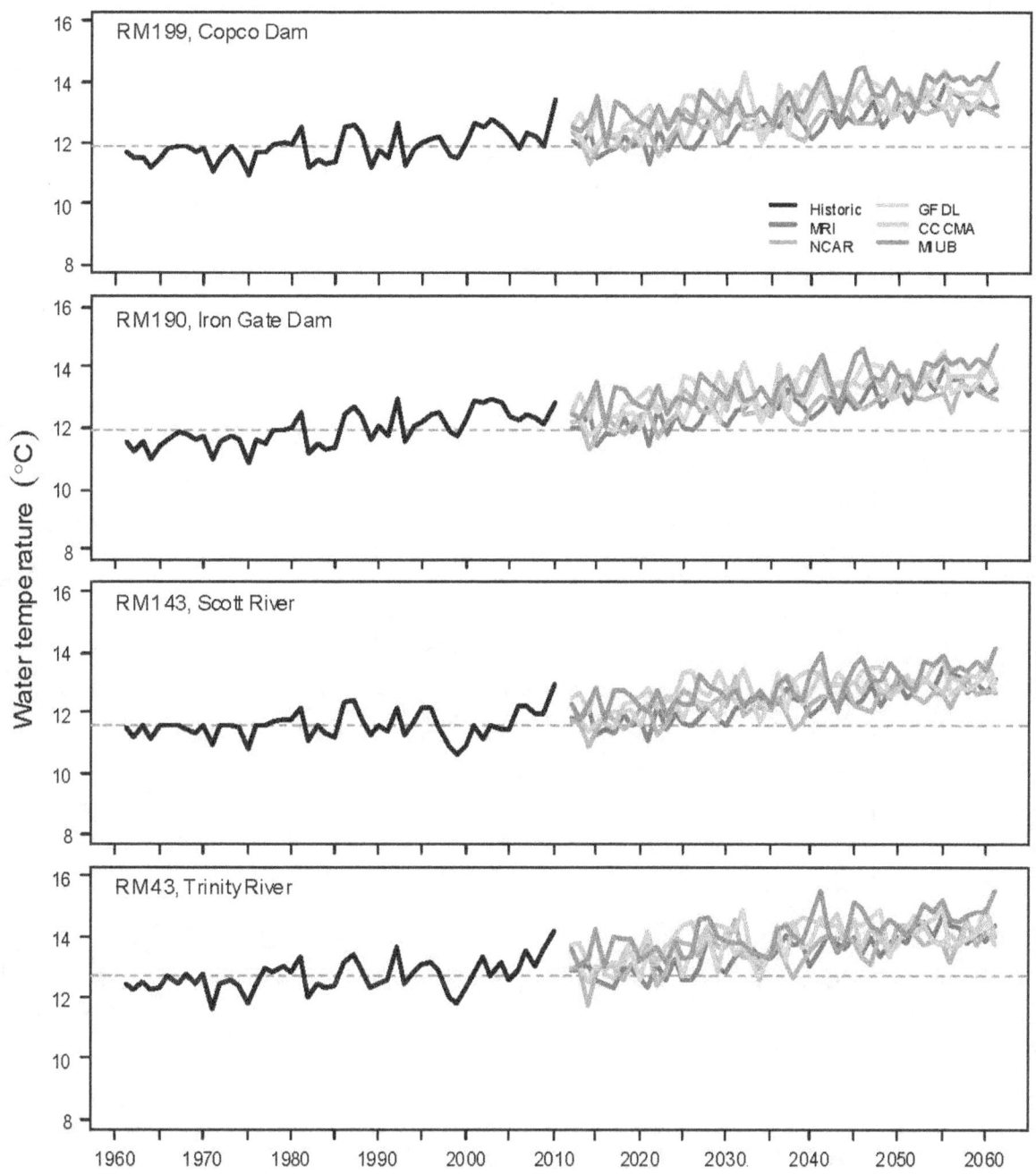

Figure 26. Time series of annual mean water temperature for the historical simulation and the five Global Circulations Models (GCMs) under the BO scenario. The dashed reference lines show the 49-year mean of the historical time series.

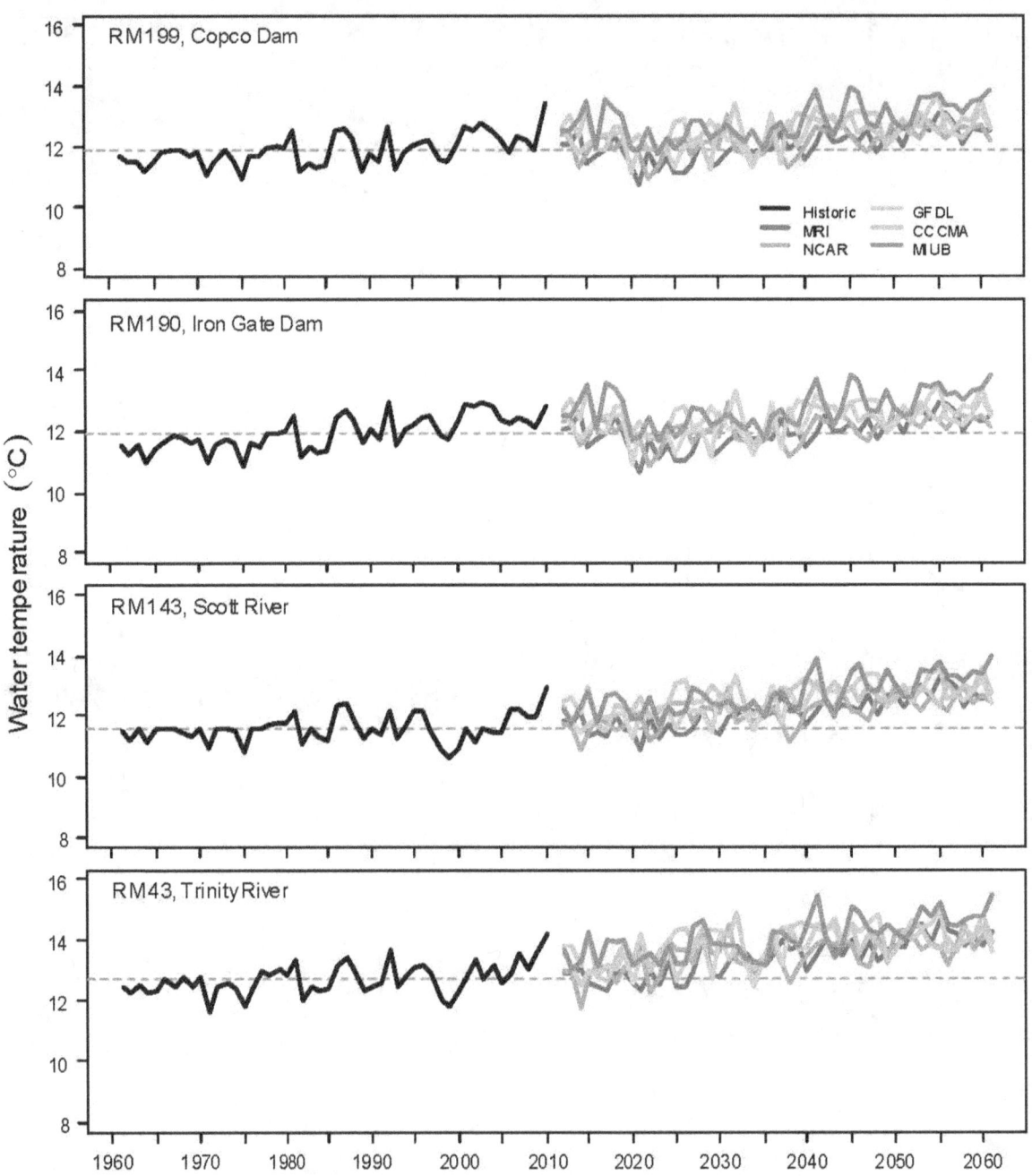

Figure 27. Time series of annual mean water temperature for the historical simulation and the five Global Circulations Models (GCMs) under the KBRA scenario. The dashed reference lines shows the 49-year mean of the historical time series.

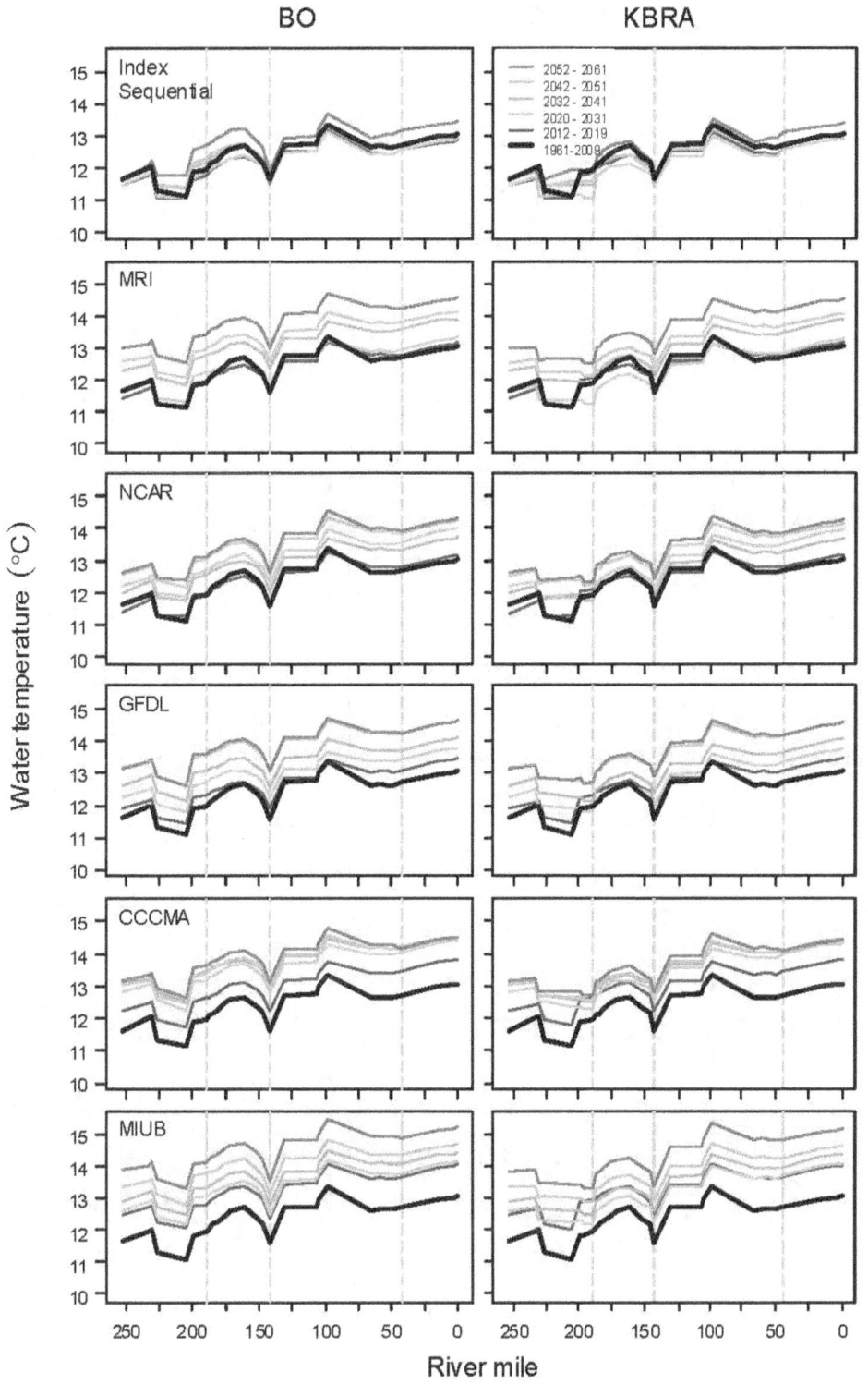

Figure 28. Mean of predicted water temperature by decade and river mile for six climate scenarios (rows) and two management scenarios (columns). Vertical reference lines mark the location of Iron Gate Dam (RM 190, RM = river mile), the Scott River (RM 142.9), and the Trinity River (RM 43.3).

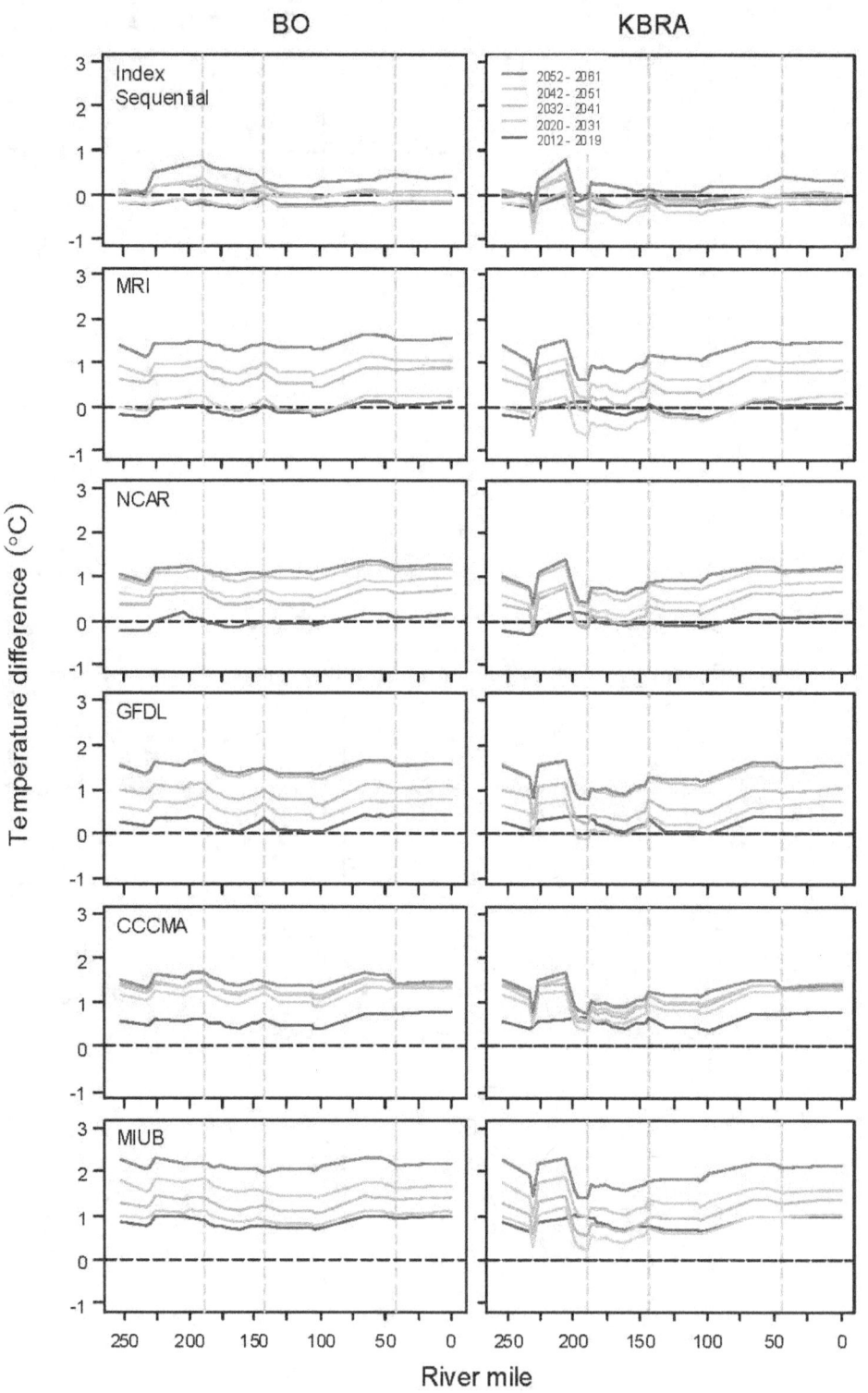

Figure 29. Difference between the decadal mean of simulated water temperature and the 49-year historical mean of simulated water temperature. Vertical reference lines mark the location of Iron Gate Dam (RM 190, RM = river mile), the Scott River (RM 142.9), and the Trinity River (RM 43.3).

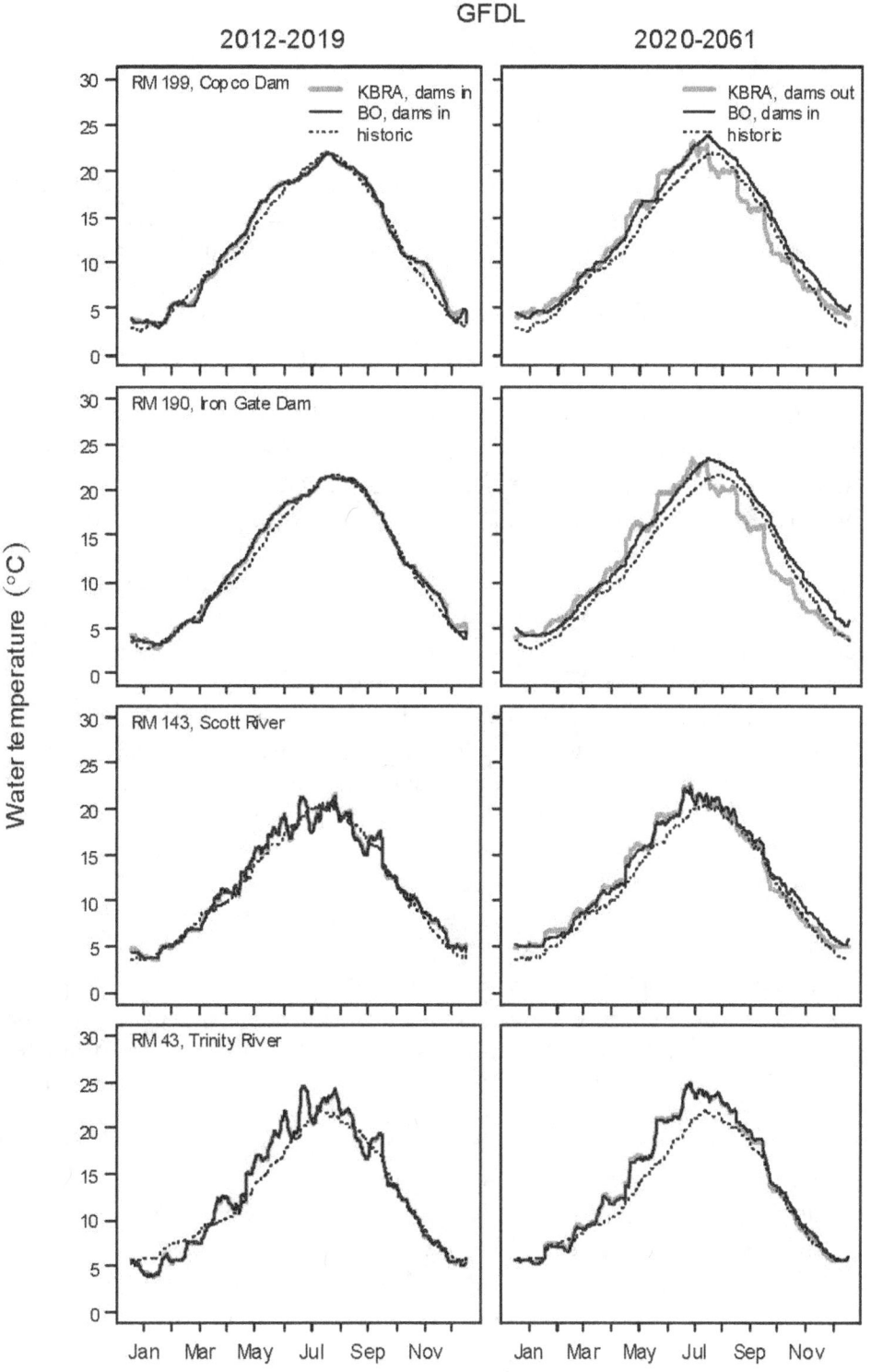

Figure 30. Mean temperature by Julian day for the KBRA dams in period (left panels) and dams out period (right panels) at four locations on the Klamath River for the GFDL General Circulation Model (GCM). The historical simulation is shown as a baseline and represents mean temperatures by Julian day for 1961–2009.

Discussion

Water temperature is a critical water quality parameter influencing fish populations, as well as the structure of the food webs on which they depend. Understanding how water temperature in the Klamath River responds to alternative water management actions is therefore a critical element in forecasting how such actions influence salmonid populations. Here, we developed a water temperature model for the Klamath River capable of simulating daily mean water temperature along the longitudinal gradient of the river between RM 253 (Link River) and the ocean. We calibrated and validated the model to an extensive set of observed water temperatures, allowing us to recreate a 49-year historical record of daily mean water temperature. The model proved useful in comparing the effects of alternative water management actions (BO and KBRA) across a range of climate scenarios. Key findings from this simulation indicated: (1) little difference in water temperature between BO and KBRA when dams were in place for both alternatives, (2) a phase shift to an earlier temperature cycle and increased variability in daily mean temperature following dam removal under KBRA in the vicinity of Iron Gate Dam, (3) little effect of dam removal downstream of the Scott River, and (4) an increase in water temperatures by 1–2.3°C due to climate change under both water management alternatives.

A limitation with a one-dimensional water temperature model is an inability to simulate potential thermal stratification in both free flowing and impounded water bodies. Although the four Klamath River dams under discussion for removal have relatively short residence times and are not used for storage, some thermal stratification exists nonetheless in the reservoirs. However, the magnitude of stratification is considerably less than that seen in large irrigation storage reservoirs in the Western United States, which typically have storage to mean annual flow volume ratios of 0.25 or greater. In those reservoirs, a thermocline typically develops in the reservoir during the spring and summer as the upper layers are warmed by solar radiation and denser cooler waters remain underneath in the hypolimnion. In the fall, when the upper layer temperatures have cooled, thermal stratification is eventually eliminated and full vertical mixing ("turnover") occurs. Reservoir drawdown for flood control or irrigation supply typically occurs in late summer or fall bringing the warmer upper layer closer to the outlet. As a consequence, river reaches downstream of deep reservoirs often have unnaturally cool and warm temperatures during the summer and fall months, respectively. In addition, annual streamflow patterns are altered as higher flows are stored and released resulting in dampened peak streamflows and augmented base flows (Risley and others, 2010).

In spite of some thermal stratification in the Klamath River reservoirs, a one-dimensional model like RBM10 was still successful in simulating the impacts of dam removal on water temperatures by accounting for changes in channel hydraulics. In RBM10, reservoirs are configured as impounded water bodies with fixed water elevations. River reaches are configured as free flowing with dynamic water elevations and surface areas. RBM10 is then able to simulate changes in thermal loading resulting from changes in the water body volume and the water surface area.

Simulated water temperatures indicated the annual temperature cycle will be shifted about 18 days earlier near Iron Gate Dam following dam removal (fig. 17). This phase shift is consistent with earlier modeling efforts by Bartholow and others (2005). The phase shift occurs because the reservoir water mass warms relatively slow as seasonal warming occurs during spring. Similarly, the warm water mass in reservoirs is slow to cool in the fall compared to free-flowing rivers, causing relatively warm water temperatures downstream of dams during fall. Several attributes of the predicted seasonal temperature cycles will likely be of importance to salmonid behavior, growth, and migration behavior as well as their relationship with disease pathogens. We examined the difference in temperature during May because salmon smolts out-migrate to the Pacific Ocean in the spring, and during October, because adult Chinook salmon return upstream to spawn in fall. The maximum temperature difference in May at

Iron Gate Dam (RM 190) averaged 2°C warmer without dams (fig. 18). During October, the maximum temperature difference at Iron Gate Dam was about 4°C cooler. Bartholow and others (2005) predicted that conditions without dams would be about 5°C cooler downstream of Iron Gate Dam compared to conditions with dams present. Bartholow and others (2005) also found that the summer maxima without dams shifted on average by 21 days, but found high variability in this shift because the river without dams was more responsive to ambient meteorological variation.

The longitudinal patterns of predicted water temperatures downstream of Iron Gate Dam varied over the season. The maximum difference between temperatures simulated for the two alternatives occurred at Iron Gate Dam and became more attenuated approaching the Klamath River estuary. The difference in simulated water temperature for dams out and dams in during May was substantially diminished (<1°C) by RM 100 at Happy Camp (fig. 18). However, during July the difference in water temperature between the alternatives was less than 1°C downstream of RM 161 at Beaver (fig 18). In October, the difference in water temperature between the alternatives was less than 1°C downstream of RM 100 at Happy Camp. The downstream differences between temperatures for the two alternatives generally are attenuated so the differences are small near the estuary. In general, Bartholow and others (2005) found the influence of upstream reservoirs was attenuated at Seiad Valley (RM 61).

Summary

A one-dimensional physically based water temperature model was developed for the Klamath River in south-central Oregon and northern California to analyze potential impacts of alternative water management plans being proposed for the Klamath Basin. In recent years, the Klamath Basin has had considerable controversy over water-related resource issues in the past and current century as agriculture, forestry, hydropower, and fish and wildlife interests have competed for scarce water resources. In 2010, the Klamath Basin stakeholders came together to sign the Klamath Hydroelectric Settlement Agreement (KHSA) and the Klamath Basin Restoration Agreement (KBRA). In the agreements, the Basin's stakeholders agreed to move forward toward removal of the lower four hydroelectric dams (J.C. Boyle, Copco 1, Copco 2, and Iron Gate) on the Klamath River, scheduled for 2020. Of interest, in this study, are the impacts of two possible future water management scenarios over a 50-year period (2012–2061). The first scenario assumes no change from the current management, which includes on-going programs under existing laws and authorities that contribute to the continued existence of listed threatened and endangered species. However, the second scenario assumes the removal of the lower four Klamath River dams in the year 2020 and implementation of the actions and restoration programs in KBRA.

The River Basin Model-10 (RBM10), the model selected for the study, is based on a heat budget formulation to predict daily water temperatures along the longitudinal profile of a river. The model's structure and associated input files can be separated into three components: (1) river geometry, (2) boundary conditions, and (3) meteorological data. The model defines system geometry as a series of reservoir or river segments. Given boundary conditions and river geometry, RBM10 uses a simple equilibrium flow model, assuming discharge in each river segment on each day is transmitted downstream instantaneously. The model uses a heat budget formulation to quantify heat flux at the air-water interface. Inputs for the heat budget are calculated from daily meteorological data, which includes: net shortwave solar radiation, net long-wave atmospheric radiation, air temperature, wind speed, vapor pressure, and a psychrometric constant needed to calculate the Bowen ratio. Cloud cover is not a direct model input, but was used in this study to calculate net shortwave and longwave radiation.

Water temperatures are then simulated using an Eulerian-Lagrangian numerical scheme that is both accurate and computationally efficient.

In the first phase of the study, the model was used to construct a 49-year historical (1961–2009) time series of water temperature in the Klamath River that could be used as a baseline against which to compare simulations of alternative management and climate change scenarios. The modeling domain, encompassing a distance of almost 250 river miles from Klamath Falls, Oregon, to near the Pacific Ocean, was divided into nine separate reaches. The nine modeling reaches, ranging in length from 10.8 to 42.4 miles, were each calibrated and validated separately using observed daily-mean water temperature data collected at their downstream ends. A set of air-water temperature statistical models were created to predict a 49-year time series (1961–2009) of daily-mean water temperature for the upstream river boundary near Klamath Falls, Oregon, and eight tributary boundaries. The only RBM10 model parameters that were adjusted during the calibration process were coefficients to wind speed, which affected the evaporative heat flux in the heat budget equation. Final calibration results yielded root mean square errors of observed versus simulated water temperatures ranging from 0.8 to 1.5°C for nine modeling reaches. Mean absolute errors ranged from 0.6 to 1.2°C. For model validation, a *k*-fold cross-validation technique was used. Validation root mean square error and mean absolute error for the nine reaches ranged from 0.8 to 1.4°C and 0.8 to 1.2°C, respectively.

RBM10 was used to simulate water temperatures for a 50-year period (2012–2061) under two management scenarios and six alternative climate scenarios (that is, twelve 50-year simulations). The six climate scenarios represent hydrology and meteorology using the "Index Sequential Method" and five alternative Global Circulation Models. The Index Sequential Method used the historical meteorology and hydrology, but was applied to the operational conditions of either BO (dams in) or KBRA (dams out). In the Index Sequential Method simulations, the largest water temperature differences between BO and KBRA occurred at Iron Gate Dam after dam removal and attenuated approaching lower reaches of the Klamath River. Simulated mean temperatures for May increased by about 2°C after dam removal near Iron Gate Dam and decreased to about a 1°C increase at the Scott River. Simulated mean temperatures for October decreased by 4°C at Iron Gate Dam, by about 2°C at the Scott River, and by less than 1°C at the Trinity River. Dam removal also resulted in an earlier annual temperature cycle shift of 18 days, 6 days, and 2 days, near Iron Gate Dam, Scott River, and Trinity River, respectively. Seasonal changes in water temperature under climate change, using the five alternative Global Circulation Models, also were similar to the Index Sequential simulation results. The main difference was that both the BO and KBRA projected temperatures typically were higher than the historical temperatures. Although the magnitude of precipitation and air temperature change predicted by the five Global Circulation Models varied between them, all five models resulted in progressive incremental increases in water temperatures with each decade from 2012 to 2061. The sum of the incremental increases for the five GCMs ranged from less than1 to greater than 2°C.

Potential changes in seasonal water temperatures resulting from dam removal under the Index Sequential Method (historical climate) scenario or under climate change are likely to have a direct impact on fisheries in the Klamath Basin. Water temperature changes in May are of particular interest because salmon smolts out-migrate to the Pacific Ocean in the spring and during October when Chinook salmon return upstream to spawn.

Acknowledgments

We are grateful to Blair Greimann and his colleagues at the Bureau of Reclamation, Denver, Colorado, for flow and climate change modeling that made this modeling effort possible. We also are indebted to Lorraine Flint and Alan Flint, USGS, Sacramento, California, for their contribution to datasets and guidance that formed a basis for the modeling. Stewart Rounds and Annette Sullivan, USGS, Portland, Oregon, graciously provided critical data for model construction and advice about calibration, validation, and model structure. We thank Chauncey Anderson, USGS and Paul Zedonis, U.S. Fish and Wildlife Service, Co-chairs of the Water Quality Subgroup for the Secretarial Determination for their assistance and constructive comments. We also want to thank Lynne Casal and our colleagues at the Columbia River Research Laboratory, Western Fisheries Research Center, USGS for their administrative support and assistance. This study was funded under an interagency agreement between the USGS and the U.S. Fish and Wildlife Service, Yreka, California.

References Cited

AgriMet, The Pacific Northwest Cooperative Agriculture Weather Network, 2011, Worden, Oregon: AgriMet Station (WRDO) weather database accessed July 20, 2011 at http://www.usbr.gov/pn/agrimet/agrimetmap/wrdoda.html.

Ångström, Anders, 1918, A study of the radiation of the atmosphere: Smithsonian Institute Miscellaneous Collection, v. 65, p. 159-161.

Bartholow, J.M., Campbell, S.G., and Flug, Marshall, 2005, Predicting the thermal effects of dam removal on the Klamath River: Environmental Management, New York, v. 34(6), p. 856-874.

California Rivers Assessment, 2011, Watershed information by basin, average precipitation per year: California Rivers Assessment, Watershed database, accessed July 21, 2011, at *http://endeavor.des.ucdavis.edu/newcara*.

Daly, C., Halbleib, M., Smith, J.I., Gibson, W.P., Doggett, M.K., Taylor, G.H., Curtis, J., and Pasteris, P.A., 2008, Physiographically-sensitive mapping of temperature and precipitation across the conterminous United States: International Journal of Climatology, v. 28, p. 2031-2064.

Davison, A.C., and Hinkley, D.V., 1997, Bootstrap methods and their application—Cambridge series in statistical and probabilistic mathematics (1st ed.): Cambridge, Cambridge University Press, UK, 592 p.

Deas, M.L., and Orlob, G.T., 1999, Klamath River Modeling Project and Appendices: Davis, California, University of California, 376 p.

Edinger, J.E., Brady, D.K., and Geyer, J.C., 1974, Heat exchange and transport in the environment: Electric Power Research Institute, Cooling Water Discharge Research Project (RP-49), 125 p.

Flerchinger, G.N., Xaio, Wei, Marks, Danny, Sauer, T.J., and Qiang, Yu, 2009, Comparison of algorithms for incoming atmospheric long-wave radiation: Water Resources Research, v. 45, 13 p.

Flint, L.E., and Flint, A.L., 2008, A basin-scale approach to estimating stream temperatures of tributaries to the Lower Klamath River, California: Journal of Environmental Quality, v. 37, 68 p.

Greimann, B.P., Varyu, D., Godaire, J., Russell, Kendra, L., Y.G., Talbot, R., and King, D., eds., 2011, Hydrology, hydraulics and sediment transport studies for the secretary's determination on Klamath River Dam removal and basin restoration: Bureau of Reclamation, Mid-Pacific Region, Technical Service Center, Denver, Colorado, Technical Report No. SRH-2011-02, 762 p.

Henderson-Sellers, B., 1986, Calculating the surface energy balance for lake and reservoir modeling—a review: Reviews of Geophysics, v. 24, no. 3, p. 625-649.

Klamath Basin Restoration Agreement, 2010, Klamath basin restoration agreement for the sustainability of public and trust resources and affected communities, February 18, 2010, 371 p.

Klamath Hydroelectric Settlement Agreement, 2010, Klamath hydroelectric settlement agreement, February 18, 2010, 208p.

King, D., Sutley, D., and Raff, D., 2011, Klamath Dam removal study climate change hydrology development, Appendix E, documentation of hydrology simulations for the Klamath Dam removal studies, Section 17.2, climate change hydrology, *of* Greimann, B.P., Varyu, D., Godaire, J., Russell, Kendra, L., Y.G., Talbot, R., and King, D., eds., 2011, Hydrology, Hydraulics and Sediment Transport Studies for the Secretary's Determination on Klamath River Dam Removal and Basin Restoration: Bureau of Reclamation, Mid-Pacific Region, Technical Service Center, Denver, Colo. Technical Report No. SRH-2011-02, 1–15.

Maurer, E.P., Wood, A.W., Adam, J.C., Lettenmaier, D.P., and Nijssen, B., 2002, A long-term hydrologically-based data set of land surface fluxes and states for the conterminous United States: Journal of Climate, v. 15, p. 3,237–3,251.

Mohseni, Omid, Stefan, H.G., and Erickson, T.R., 1998, A nonlinear regression model for weekly stream temperatures: Water Resources Research, v. 34, no. 10, p. 2,685–2,692.

National Marine Fisheries Service, 2010, Biological opinion, Operation of the Klamath project between 2010 and 2018: National Marine Fisheries Service, Southwest Region, File No. 151422SWR2008AR00148, 226 p.

Oregon Department of Environmental Quality, 2011, Water quality assessment database: Oregon 2004/2006 Integrated Report, database accessed May 25, 2011 at *http://www.deq.state.or.us/wq/assessment/rpt0406/results.asp.*

PacifiCorp, 2004, Final Technical Report – Klamath Hydroelectric Project, FERC Project No. 2082, Water Resources.

R Development Core Team, 2010, R—a language and environment for statistical computing: R Foundation for Statistical Computing, ISBN 3-900051-07-0, accessed Sept. 13, 2011, at *http://www.r-project.org/.*

Risley, J.C., Constantz, J., Essaid, H., and Rounds, S., 2010, Effects of upstream dams versus groundwater pumping on stream temperature under varying climate conditions: Water Resources Research, v. 46, 32 p.

Rymer, R., 2008, Reuniting a river: Klamath Forest Alliance, accessed Sept. 13, 2011, at *http://www.klamathforestalliance.org/Newsarticles/newsarticle20081201.html.*

Sullivan, A.B., Rounds, S.A., Deas, M.L., Asbill, J.R., Wellman, R.E., Stewart, M.A., Johnston, M.W., and Sogutlugil, I.E., 2011, Modeling hydrodynamics, water temperature, and water quality in the Klamath River upstream of Keno Dam, Oregon, 2006-09: U.S. Geological Survey Scientific Investigations Report 2011-5105, 70 p. (Also available at *http://pubs.usgs.gov/sir/2011/5105/.*)

Turaski, 2003, 2002 and 2003 Upper Klamath River water temperature monitoring: Bureau of Land Management, Lakeview District, Klamath Falls Resource area, 19 p.

Unsworth, M.H., and Monteith, J.L., 1975, Long-wave radiation at the ground I. Angular distribution of the incoming radiation: Quarterly Journal of the Royal Meteorological Society, v. 101, p. 13–24.

University of Washington, Department of Civil and Environmental Engineering Surface Water Modeling Group, Seattle, Washington: Gridded Meteorological database accessed July 20, 2011 at *http://www.hydro.washington.edu/Lettenmaier/Data/gridded/index_maurer.html.*

U.S. Army Corps of Engineers, 2010, HEC-RAS—River Analysis System, User's Manual Version 4.1, January 2010, CPD-68: U.S. Army Corps of Engineers, Institute for Water Resources, Hydrological Engineering Center (HEC), 790 p., accessed September 13, 2011 at *www.hec.usace.army.mil.*

U.S. Department of the Interior, Bureau of Reclamation, 2008, Sensitivity of Future CVP/SWP Operations to Potential Climate Change and Associated Sea Level Rise, Appendix R in: Biological Assessment on Continued Long-term Operations of the Central Valley Project and the State Water Project, 135 p.

U.S. Department of the Interior, Bureau of Reclamation, San Joaquin River Restoration Program, 2009, Sensitivity of Future Central Valley Project and State Water Project Operations to Potential Climate Change and Associated Sea Level Rise, First Administrative Draft supplemental Hydrologic and Water Operations Analyses, Appendix. 110 p.

U.S. Fish and Wildlife Service, 2008, Biological conference opinion regarding the effects of the U.S. Bureau of Reclamation's proposed 10-year operation plan (April 1, 2008-March 31, 2018) for the Klamath Project and its effects on the endangered Lost River and shortnose suckers, April 2: Klamath Falls, Oregon, U.S. Fish and Wildlife Service, p. 197.

Weddell, B.J., 2000, Relationship between flows in the Klamath River and Lower Klamath Lake prior to 1910: U. S. Department of Interior Fish and Wildlife Service Klamath Basin Refuges, Tulelake, California, 15 p.

Willey, R.G., 1987, Water Quality Modeling of Reservoir System Operations Using HEC-5: U.S. Army Corps of Engineers, No. TD-24, 124 p.

Yearsley, John, 2003, Developing a temperature total maximum daily load for the Columbia and Snake rivers, simulation methods: Report 901-R-03-003 prepared by the U. S. Environmental Protection Agency, Region 10, Seattle, Washington, 30 p.

Yearsley, John, 2009, A semi-Lagrangian water temperature model for advection-dominated river systems: Water Resources Research, v. 45, 19 p.

Yearsley, John, Karna, Duane, Peene, Steve, and Watson, Brian, 2001, Application of a 1-D heat budget model to the Columbia River system: U.S. Environmental Protection Agency, Region 10 Final report 901-R-01-001, Seattle, Washington.

Appendix A. River Geometry, Time Series and Water Temperatures, Prediction Error, Mean Temperature for Dams In and Dams Out

Table A1. River geometry used in RBM10 for the Klamath River with all dams in place.

Segment description	Type	Start mile	End mile	Model reach	Volume (acre-ft)	Area (acres)	a_A	b_A	a_W	b_W	Tributary name	River mile
Link River to Keno	Reservoir	253.0	252.3	1	1539.248	192.088	--	--	--	--	--	--
		252.3	251.7	1	677.877	96.662	--	--	--	--	--	--
		251.7	251.1	1	570.388	77.732	--	--	--	--	--	--
		251.1	250.5	1	573.865	63.738	--	--	--	--	--	--
		250.5	250.0	1	400.362	49.798	--	--	--	--	--	--
		250.0	249.2	1	460.256	71.953	--	--	--	--	--	--
		249.2	248.6	1	474.733	58.015	--	--	--	--	--	--
		248.6	248.0	1	535.078	47.798	--	--	--	--	--	--
		248.0	247.5	1	472.958	43.702	--	--	--	--	--	--
		247.5	246.9	1	478.816	38.384	--	--	--	--	--	--
		246.9	246.1	1	752.339	63.84	--	--	--	--	--	--
		246.1	245.5	1	564.387	48.378	--	--	--	--	--	--
		245.5	244.9	1	600.562	57.554	--	--	--	--	--	--
		244.9	244.3	1	623.98	64.19	--	--	--	--	--	--
		244.3	243.7	1	649.626	69.627	--	--	--	--	--	--
		243.7	243.1	1	624.738	66.579	--	--	--	--	--	--
		243.1	242.4	1	704.837	67.814	--	--	--	--	--	--
		242.4	241.8	1	602.915	67.227	--	--	--	--	--	--
		241.8	241.2	1	553.539	55.713	--	--	--	--	--	--
		241.2	240.7	1	463.995	38.976	--	--	--	--	Canals	241.0
		240.7	239.9	1	534.797	40.656	--	--	--	--	--	--
		239.9	239.4	1	422.823	32.515	--	--	--	--	--	--
		239.4	238.8	1	537.448	46.398	--	--	--	--	--	--
		238.8	238.0	1	733.69	64.303	--	--	--	--	--	--
		238.0	237.4	1	492.184	43.158	--	--	--	--	--	--
		237.4	236.9	1	479.459	39.482	--	--	--	--	--	--
		236.9	236.3	1	471.85	40.657	--	--	--	--	--	--
		236.3	235.7	1	470.485	40.554	--	--	--	--	--	--
		235.7	235.0	1	541.681	41.86	--	--	--	--	--	--
		235.0	234.4	1	295.296	40.473	--	--	--	--	--	--
		234.4	233.8	1	378.62	48.97	--	--	--	--	--	--
		233.8	233.4	1	289.218	28.893	--	--	--	--	--	--
Keno to JC Boyle	River	233.4	230.3	1	--	--	3.498	0.631	156.906	0.060	--	--

JC Boyle Reservoir	Reservoir	230.3	229.7	2	245.615	56.558	--	--	--	--	--	--
		229.7	229.0	2	866.911	193.198	--	--	--	--	--	--
		229.0	228.3	2	995.571	154.871	--	--	--	--	--	--
		228.3	227.6	2	480.228	51.684	--	--	--	--	--	--
		227.6	226.9	2	1263.331	76.68	--	--	--	--	Spencer Cr	227.5
JC Boyle to Copcol-A	River	226.9	222.2	2	--	--	1.636	0.678	33.235	0.164	--	--
JC Boyle to Copcol-B	River	222.2	216.2	2	--	--	3.364	0.650	69.435	0.144	Boyle Sp	222.0
JC Boyle to Copcol-C	River	216.2	212.2	2	--	--	2.111	0.656	53.567	0.131	Shovel Cr	206.4
JC Boyle to Copcol-D	River	212.2	205.2	2	--	--	2.584	0.689	29.512	0.265	--	--
Copcol Reservoir	Reservoir	205.2	204.6	2	169.273	23.094	--	--	--	--	--	--
		204.6	203.9	2	800.139	74.586	--	--	--	--	--	--
		203.9	203.3	2	1707.061	112.78	--	--	--	--	--	--
		203.3	202.6	2	3029.531	144.729	--	--	--	--	--	--
		202.6	202	2	6181.262	205.666	--	--	--	--	--	--
		202.0	201.3	2	6975.880	175.608	--	--	--	--	--	--
		201.3	200.7	2	14132.477	286.409	--	--	--	--	--	--
		200.7	200	2	13078.434	320.214	--	--	--	--	--	--
		200.0	199.2	2	12515.242	200.746	--	--	--	--	--	--
Copcol Reservoir	Reservoir	199.2	198.9	2	1123.646	16.986	--	--	--	--	--	--
Copcol to Iron Gate	River	198.9	197.2	2	--	--	1.650	0.681	18.609	0.231	--	--
Iron Gate Reservoir	Reservoir	197.2	196.6	2	88.563	14.026	--	--	--	--	--	--
		196.6	195.9	2	783.598	55.662	--	--	--	--	--	--
		195.9	195.2	2	1283.183	52.318	--	--	--	--	--	--
		195.2	194.5	2	2852.553	80.323	--	--	--	--	--	--
		194.5	193.9	2	4144.604	105.156	--	--	--	--	Jenny Cr	194.1
		193.9	193.3	2	3284.823	68.214	--	--	--	--	--	--
		193.3	192.6	2	5714.170	111.111	--	--	--	--	--	--
		192.6	191.9	2	11115.901	187.471	--	--	--	--	--	--
		191.9	191.2	2	13883.345	176.64	--	--	--	--	--	--
		191.2	190.5	2	12014.304	154.7	--	--	--	--	--	--
		190.5	190.1	2	3551.986	37.278	--	--	--	--	--	--
IG-Bogus	River	190.1	189.6	2	--	--	3.021	0.673	78.307	0.102	--	--
Bogus-Willow	River	189.6	185.0	3	--	--	3.959	0.648	29.264	0.226	--	--
Willow-Cottonwood	River	185.0	182.1	3	--	--	4.864	0.632	45.759	0.182	--	--
Cottonwood-Shasta	River	182.1	176.7	3	--	--	6.176	0.606	40.374	0.183	--	--
Shasta-Humbug	River	176.7	171.5	3	--	--	4.894	0.627	25.072	0.230	Shasta R	176.6

Humbug-Beaver	River	171.5	161.0	3	--	6.427	0.596	23.871	0.233	--	--	--
Beaver-Dona	River	161.0	152.8	3	--	4.811	0.621	22.759	0.245	--	--	--
Dona-Horse	River	152.8	147.3	4	--	3.825	0.642	22.771	0.272	--	--	--
Horse-Scott	River	147.3	143.0	4	--	3.489	0.648	51.701	0.151	--	--	--
Scott-Seiad	River	143.0	130.8	4	--	5.912	0.591	54.622	0.157	Scott R	142.9	--
Seiad-Indian	River	130.8	106.8	5	--	8.294	0.582	61.280	0.144	--	--	--
Indian-Elk	River	106.8	105.5	5	--	7.769	0.584	50.326	0.153	--	--	--
Elk-Clear	River	105.5	98.6	5	--	33.782	0.439	121.712	0.086	--	--	--
Clear-Salmon	River	98.6	66.0	6	--	1.284	0.737	18.546	0.213	--	--	--
Salmon-Orleans	River	66.0	59.2	6	--	7.126	0.600	88.005	0.095	Salmon R	65.9	--
Orleans-Red Cap	River	59.2	53.6	6	--	0.970	0.769	11.382	0.262	--	--	--
Red Cap-Bluff	River	53.6	49.5	7	--	5.737	0.625	38.048	0.165	--	--	--
Bluff-Trinity	River	49.5	43.4	7	--	3.046	0.681	61.557	0.121	--	--	--
Trinity-Blue	River	43.4	16.1	8	--	2.751	0.688	12.493	0.265	Trinity R	43.3	--
Blue-Klamath	River	16.1	2.8	9	--	8.709	0.631	142.613	0.079	--	--	--
Klamath-Ocean	River	2.8.0	0.0	9	--	18.345	0.580	507.633	0.020	--	--	--

Table A2. River geometry used in RBM10 for the Klamath River with the four lower dams removed.

Segment description	Type	Start mile	End mile	Model reach	Volume (acre-ft)	Area (acres)	a_A	b_A	a_W	b_W	Tributary name	River mile
Link River to Keno	Reservoir	253.0	252.3	1	1539.248	192.088	--	--	--	--	--	--
		252.3	251.7	1	677.877	96.662	--	--	--	--	--	--
		251.7	251.1	1	570.388	77.732	--	--	--	--	--	--
		251.1	250.5	1	573.865	63.738	--	--	--	--	--	--
		250.5	250.0	1	400.362	49.798	--	--	--	--	--	--
		250.0	249.2	1	460.256	71.953	--	--	--	--	--	--
		249.2	248.6	1	474.733	58.015	--	--	--	--	--	--
		248.6	248.0	1	535.078	47.798	--	--	--	--	--	--
		248.0	247.5	1	472.958	43.702	--	--	--	--	--	--
		247.5	246.9	1	478.816	38.384	--	--	--	--	--	--
		246.9	246.1	1	752.339	63.840	--	--	--	--	--	--
		246.1	245.5	1	564.387	48.378	--	--	--	--	--	--
		245.5	244.9	1	600.562	57.554	--	--	--	--	--	--
		244.9	244.3	1	623.980	64.190	--	--	--	--	--	--
		244.3	243.7	1	649.626	69.627	--	--	--	--	--	--
		243.7	243.1	1	624.738	66.579	--	--	--	--	--	--
		243.1	242.4	1	704.837	67.814	--	--	--	--	--	--
		242.4	241.8	1	602.915	67.227	--	--	--	--	--	--
		241.8	241.2	1	553.539	55.713	--	--	--	--	--	--
		241.2	240.7	1	463.995	38.976	--	--	--	--	Canals	241
		240.7	239.9	1	534.797	40.656	--	--	--	--	--	--
		239.9	239.4	1	422.823	32.515	--	--	--	--	--	--
		239.4	238.8	1	537.448	46.398	--	--	--	--	--	--
		238.8	238.0	1	733.690	64.303	--	--	--	--	--	--
		238.0	237.4	1	492.184	43.158	--	--	--	--	--	--
		237.4	236.9	1	479.459	39.482	--	--	--	--	--	--
		236.9	236.3	1	471.850	40.657	--	--	--	--	--	--
		236.3	235.7	1	470.485	40.554	--	--	--	--	--	--
		235.7	235.0	1	541.681	41.860	--	--	--	--	--	--
		235.0	234.4	1	295.296	40.473	--	--	--	--	--	--
		234.4	233.8	1	378.620	48.970	--	--	--	--	--	--
		233.8	233.4	1	289.218	28.893	--	--	--	--	--	--
Keno to JC Boyle	River	233.4	230.3	1	--	--	3.298	0.637	136.412	0.637	--	--
JC Boyle		230.3	226.9	1	--	--	9.746	0.599	29.830	0.599	Spencer Cr	227.5
JC Boyle to Copco1-A		226.9	222.2	1	--	--	1.470	0.688	32.866	0.688	--	--
JC Boyle to Copco1-B		222.2	216.2	1	--	--	3.227	0.657	61.016	0.657	Boyle Sp	222
JC Boyle to Copco1-C		216.2	212.2	1	--	--	2.039	0.662	51.959	0.662	Shovel Cr	206.4
JC Boyle to Copco1-D		212.2	205.2	1	--	--	2.619	0.688	32.601	0.688	--	--
Copco1		205.2	198.9	2	--	--	9.916	0.573	33.444	0.573	--	--

60

Copco to Iron Gate	198.9	197.2	2	--	--	1.715	0.686	19.262	0.686	--	--	--
Iron Gate	197.2	190.1	2	--	--	5.058	0.623	30.355	0.623	Jenny Cr	--	194.1
IG-Bogus	190.1	189.6	2	--	--	3.021	0.673	78.307	0.102	--	--	--
Bogus-Willow	189.6	185.0	3	--	--	3.959	0.648	29.264	0.226	--	--	--
Willow-Cottonwood	185.0	182.1	3	--	--	4.864	0.632	45.759	0.182	--	--	--
Cottonwood-Shasta	182.1	176.7	3	--	--	6.176	0.606	40.374	0.183	--	--	--
Shasta-Humbug	176.7	171.5	3	--	--	4.894	0.627	25.072	0.230	Shasta R	--	176.6
Humbug-Beaver	171.5	161.0	3	--	--	6.427	0.596	23.871	0.233	--	--	--
Beaver-Dona	161.0	152.8	3	--	--	4.811	0.621	22.759	0.245	--	--	--
Dona-Horse	152.8	147.3	4	--	--	3.825	0.642	22.771	0.272	--	--	--
Horse-Scott	147.3	143.0	4	--	--	3.489	0.648	51.701	0.151	--	--	--
Scott-Seiad	143	130.8	4	--	--	5.912	0.591	54.622	0.157	Scott R	--	142.9
Seiad-Indian	130.8	106.8	5	--	--	8.294	0.582	61.280	0.144	--	--	--
Indian-Elk	106.8	105.5	5	--	--	7.769	0.584	50.326	0.153	--	--	--
Elk-Clear	105.5	98.6	5	--	--	33.782	0.439	121.712	0.086	--	--	--
Clear-Salmon	98.6	66.0	6	--	--	1.284	0.737	18.546	0.213	--	--	--
Salmon-Orleans	66.0	59.2	6	--	--	7.126	0.600	88.005	0.095	Salmon R	--	65.9
Orleans-Red Cap	59.2	53.6	6	--	--	0.970	0.769	11.382	0.262	--	--	--
Red Cap-Bluff	53.6	49.5	7	--	--	5.737	0.625	38.048	0.165	--	--	--
Bluff-Trinity	49.5	43.4	7	--	--	3.046	0.681	61.557	0.121	--	--	--
Trinity-Blue	43.4	16.1	8	--	--	2.751	0.688	12.493	0.265	Trinity R	--	43.3
Blue-Klamath	16.1	2.8	9	--	--	8.709	0.631	142.613	0.079	--	--	--
Klamath-Ocean	2.8	0.0	9	--	--	18.345	0.580	507.633	0.020	--	--	--

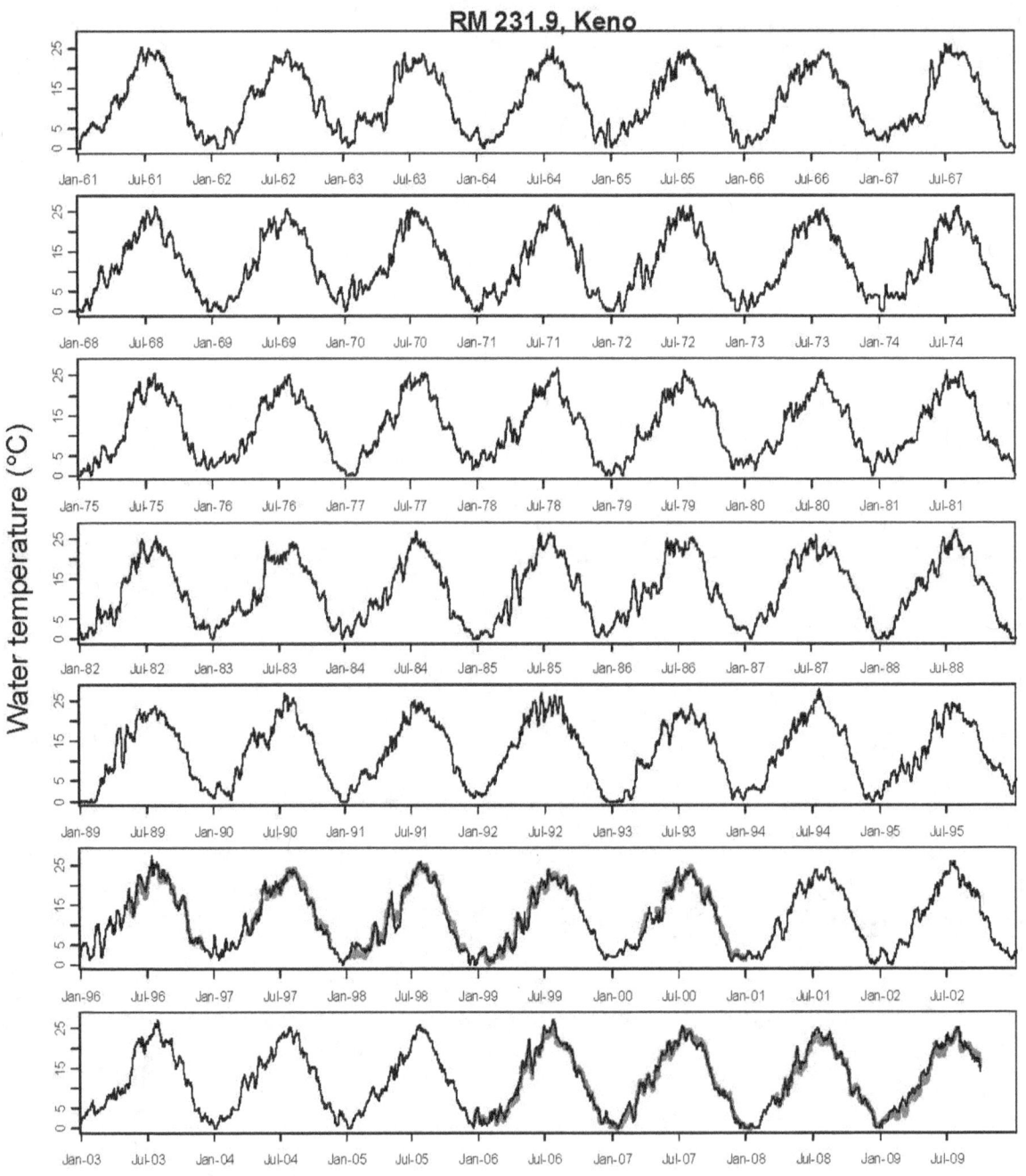

Figure A1. Time series of predicted (solid line) and observed water temperature (o) of the Klamath River at river mile (RM) 231.9.

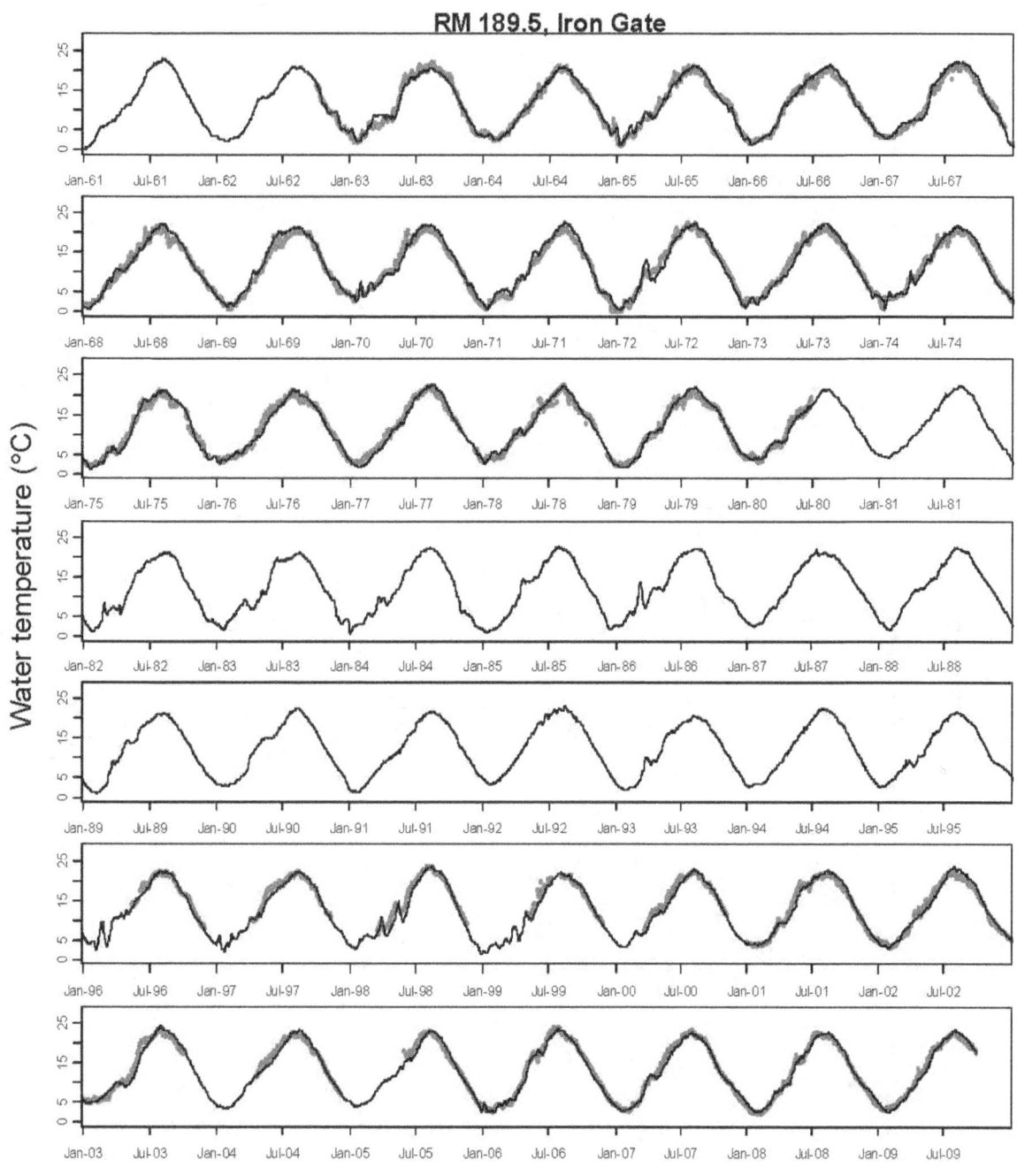

Figure A2. Time series of predicted (solid line) and observed water temperature (o) of the Klamath River at river mile (RM) 189.5.

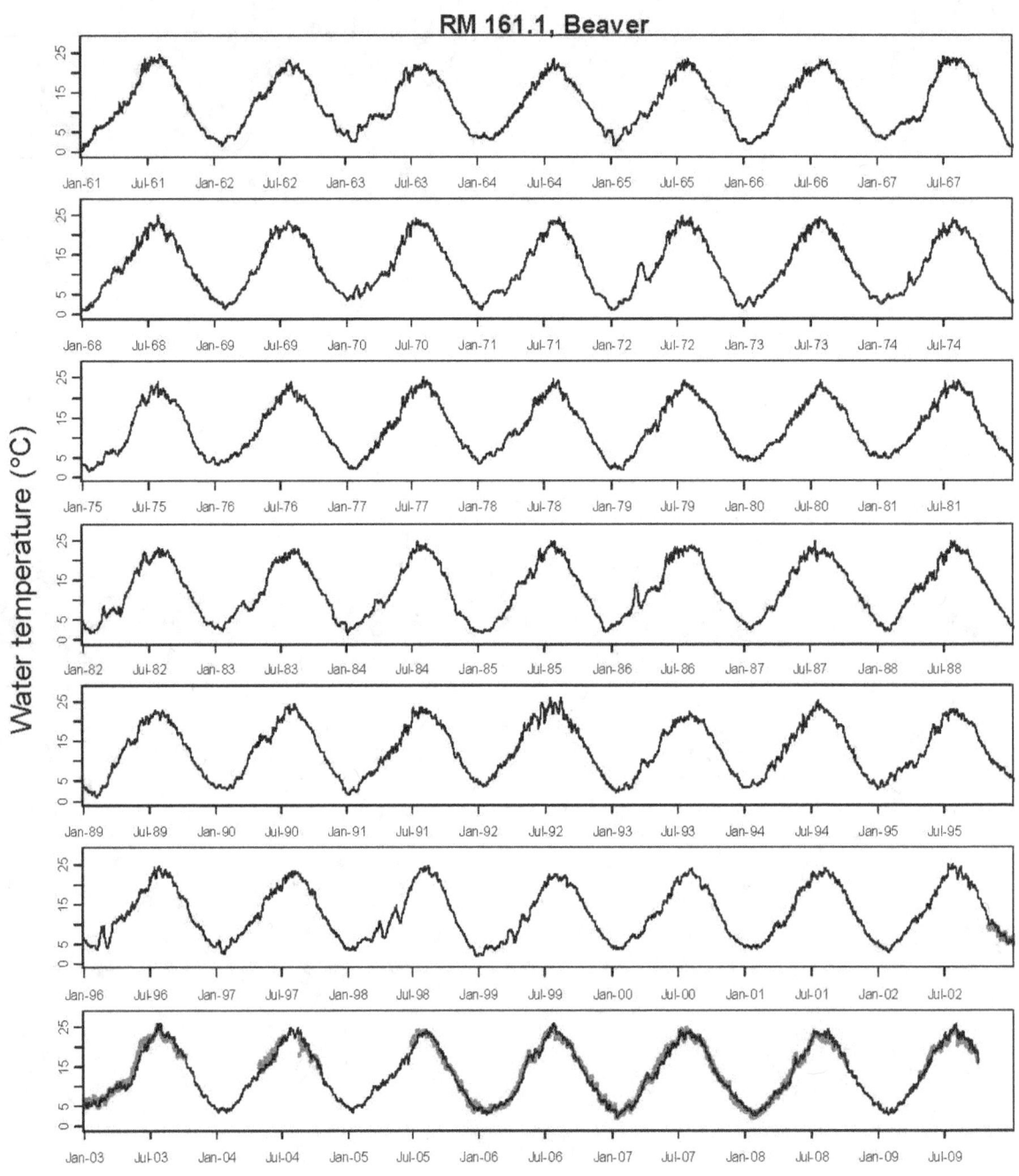

Figure A3. Time series of predicted (solid line) and observed water temperature (o) of the Klamath River at river mile (RM) 161.1.

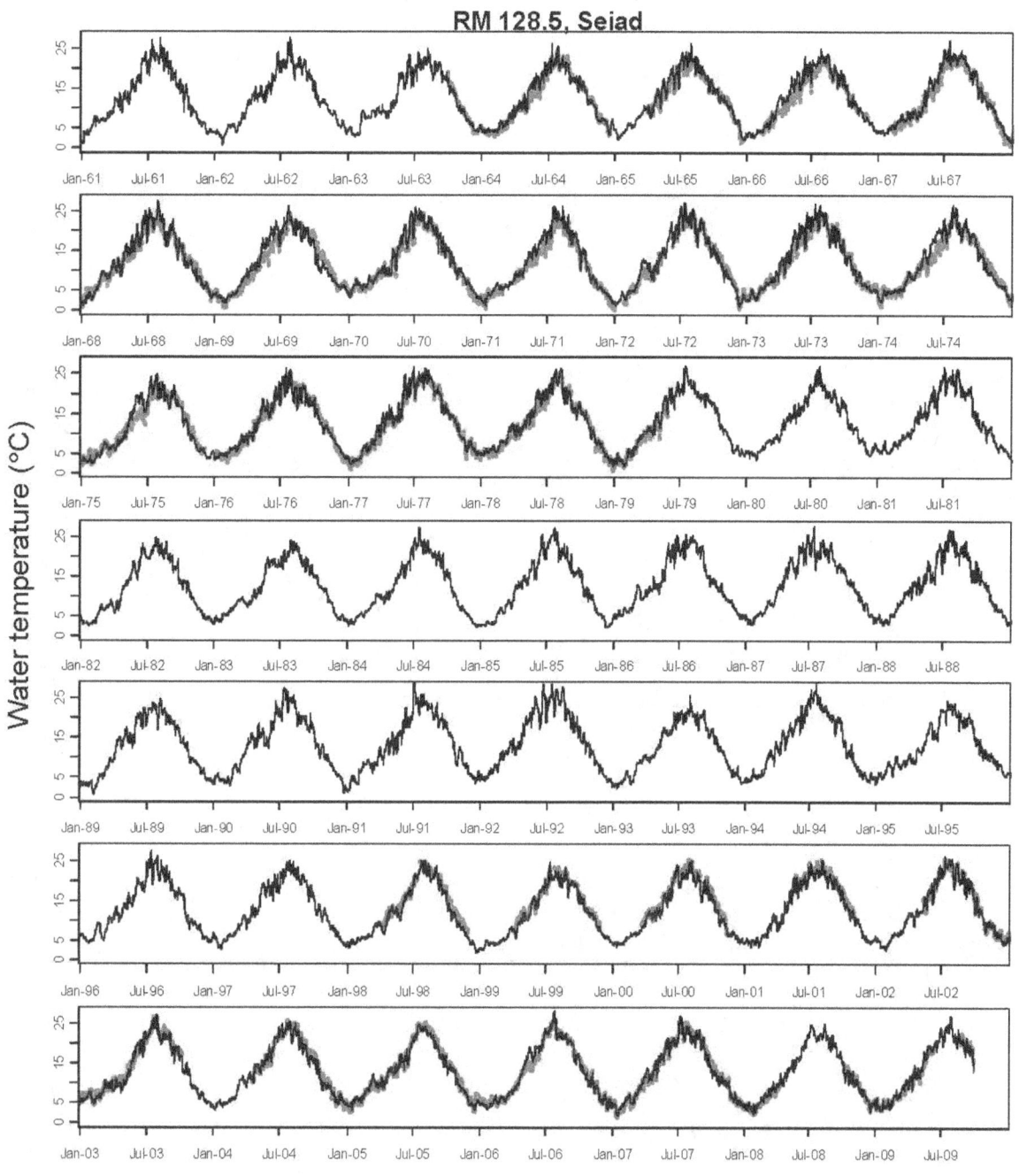

Figure A4. Time series of predicted (solid line) and observed water temperature (o) of the Klamath River at river mile (RM) 128.5.

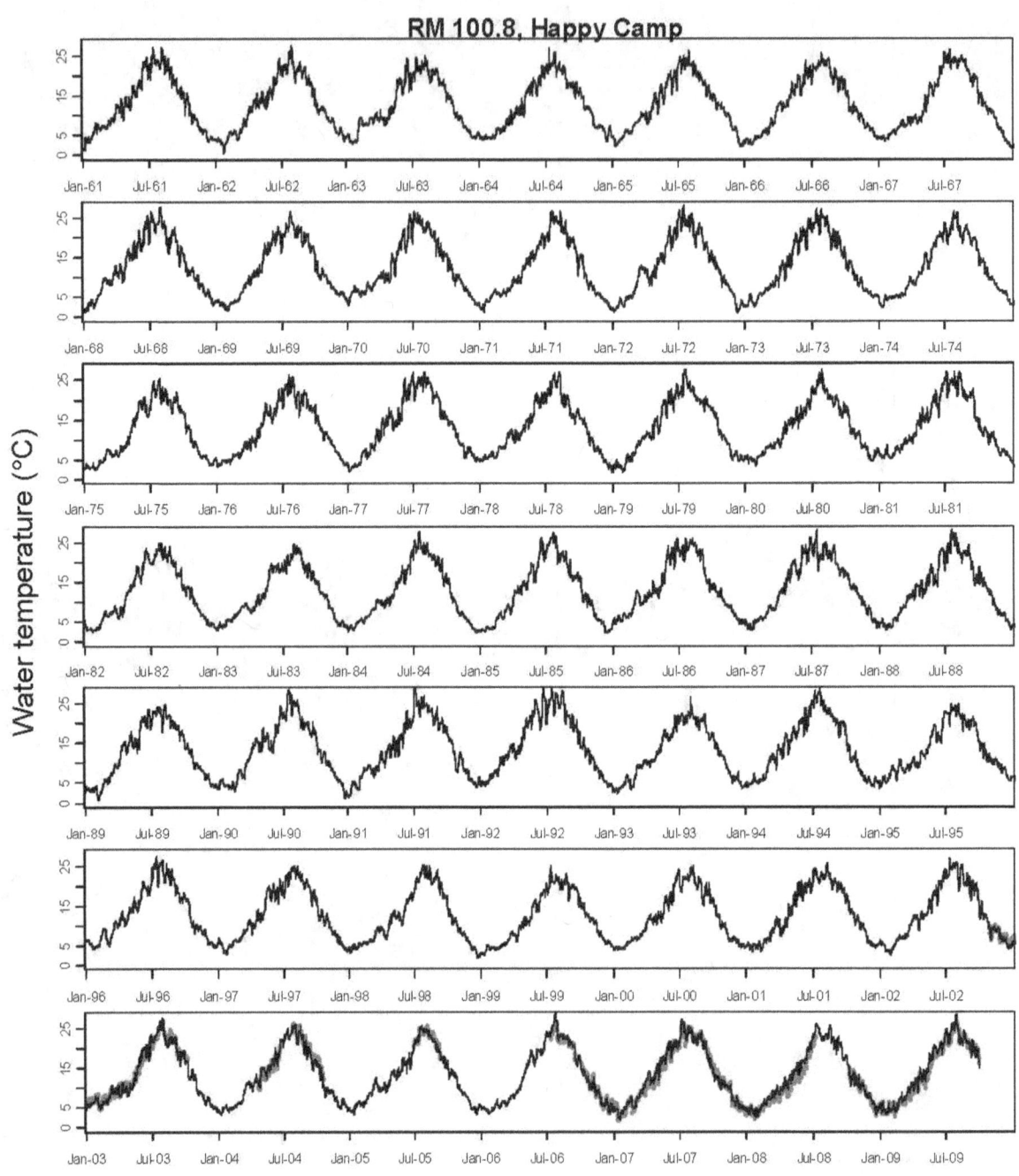

Figure A5. Time series of predicted (solid line) and observed water temperature (o) of the Klamath River at river mile (RM) 100.8.

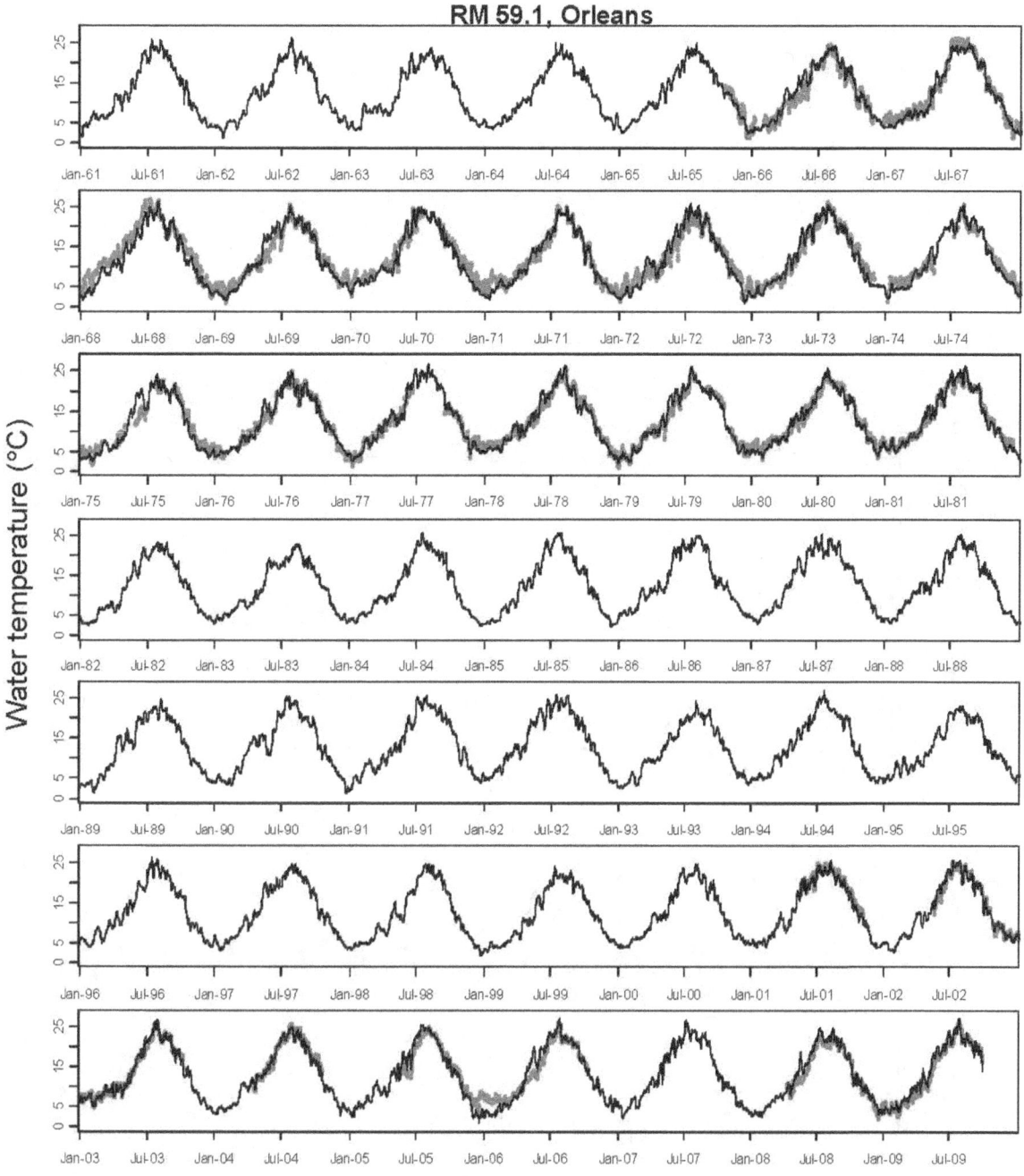

Figure A6. Time series of predicted (solid line) and observed water temperature (o) of the Klamath River at river mile (RM) 59.1.

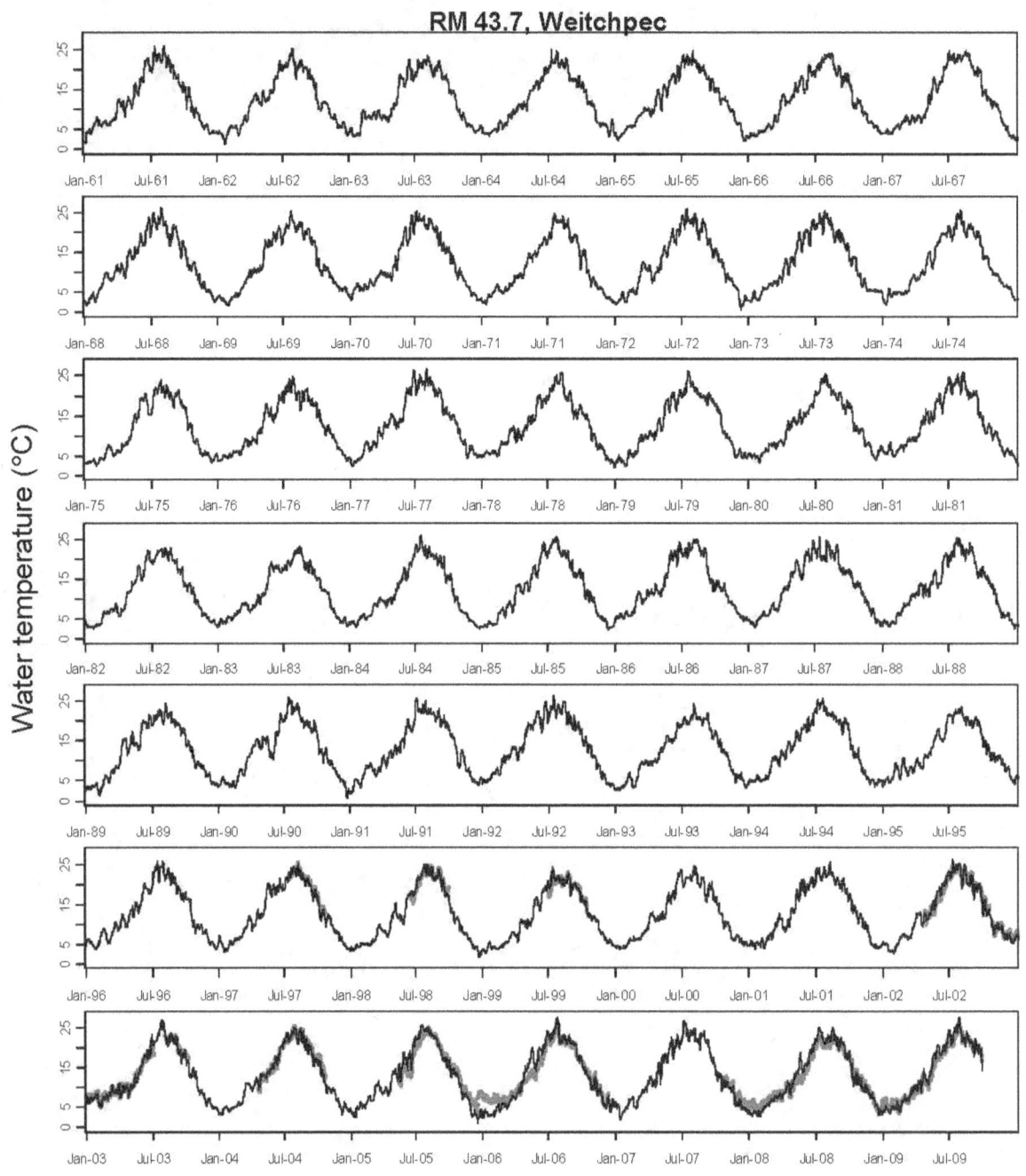

Figure A7. Time series of predicted (solid line) and observed water temperature (o) of the Klamath River at river mile (RM) 43.7.

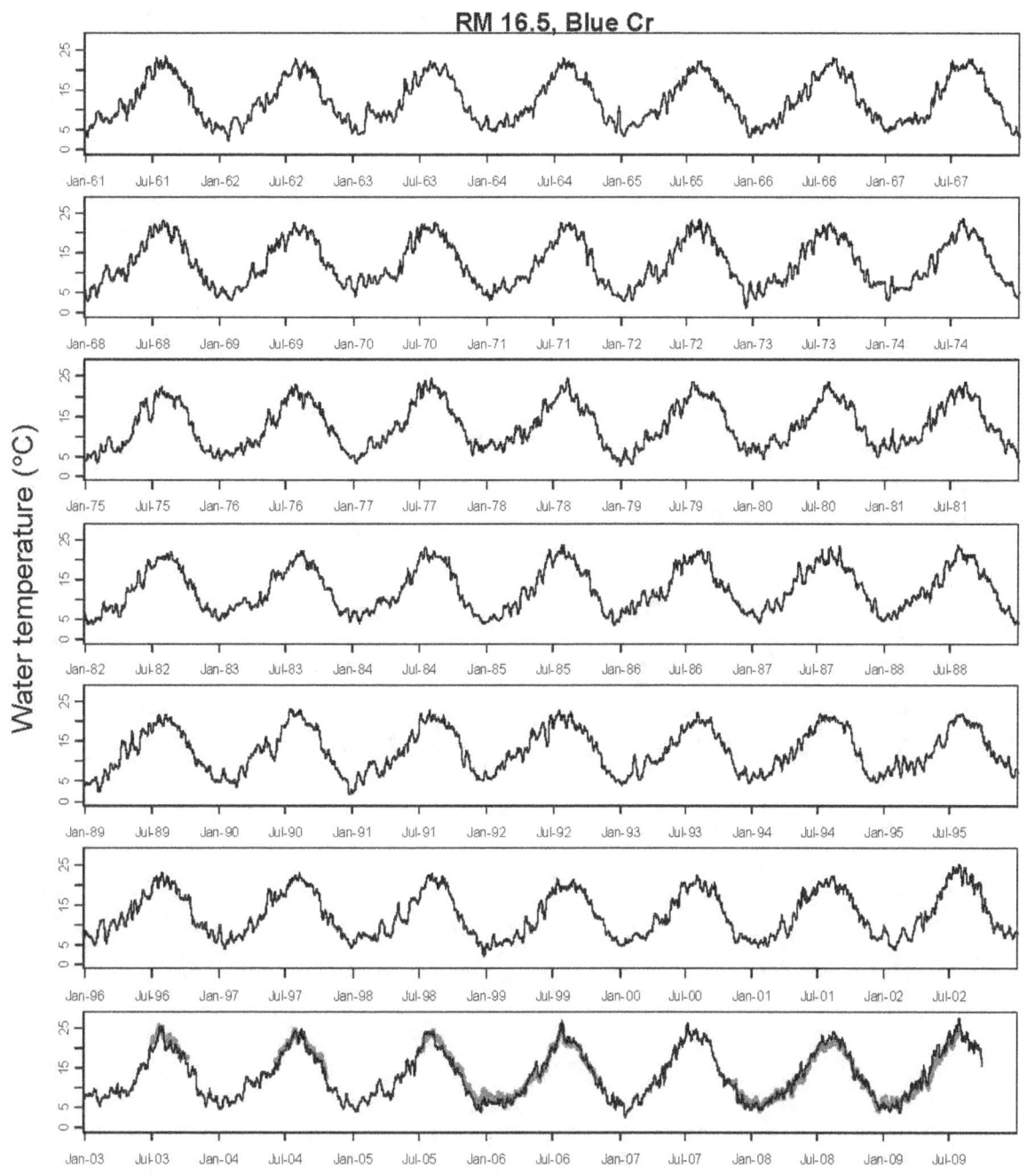

Figure A8. Time series of predicted (solid line) and observed water temperature (o) of the Klamath River at river mile (RM) 16.5.

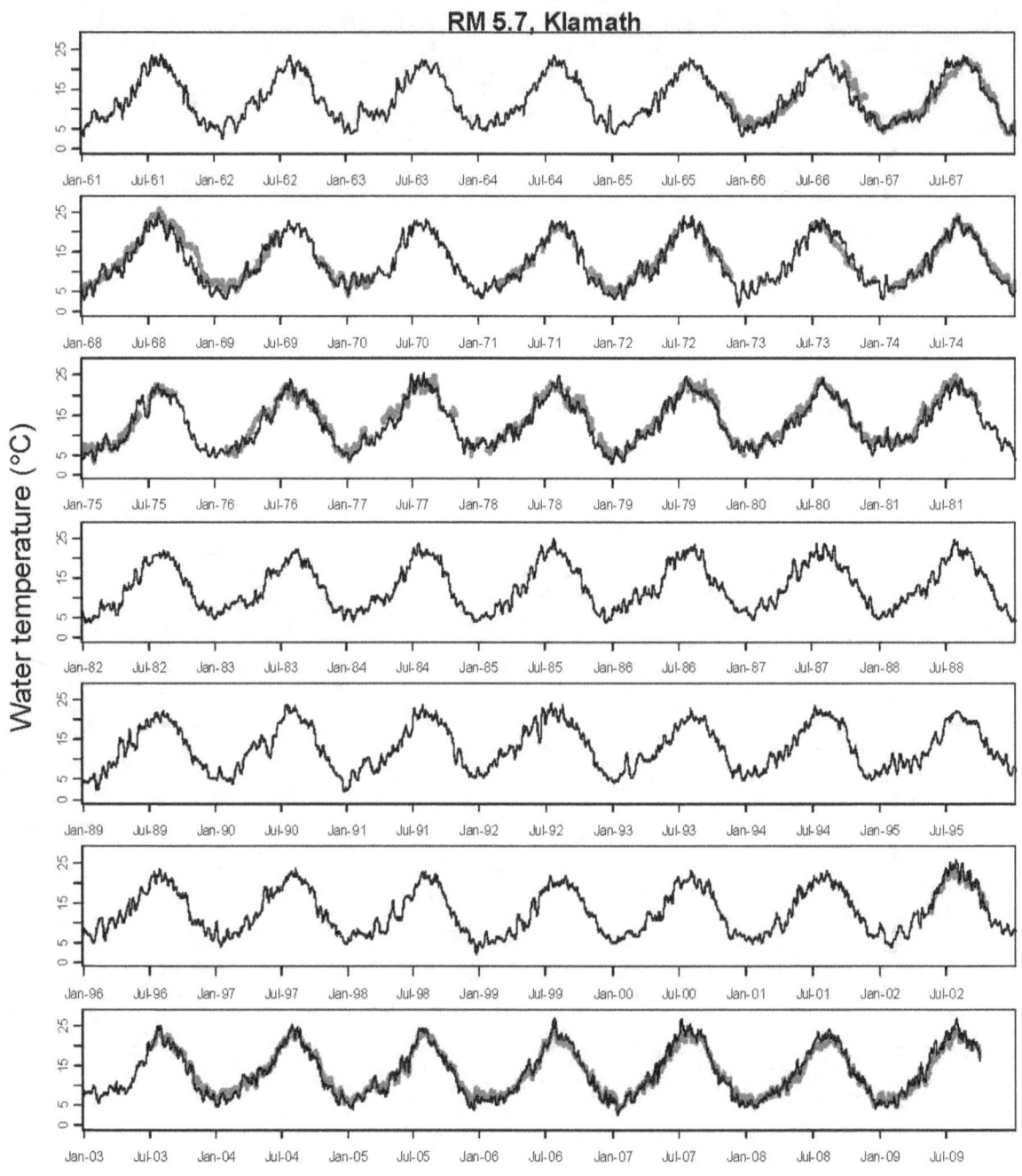

Figure A9. Time series of predicted (solid line) and observed water temperature (o) of the Klamath River at river mile (RM) 5.7.

Table A3. Year-specific prediction error from the k-fold cross-validation.
[Prediction error is estimated by calibrating to observed data without year k and then predicting water temperature in year k. Statistics are as follows: n = number of days with observed water temperature data, SS = sum of squares, NSS = Nash-Sutcliffe statistic, RMSE = root mean square error, ME = mean error, MAE = mean absolute error]

Reach (r)	Year (k)	n	SS	NSS	RMSE	ME	MAE
1	1996	179	173.01	0.971	0.983	0.337	0.734
	1997	213	172.65	0.969	0.900	-0.460	0.737
	1998	308	548.59	0.967	1.335	-0.390	1.059
	1999	253	255.81	0.983	1.006	-0.257	0.824
	2000	244	338.14	0.974	1.177	-0.825	1.008
	2005	11	1.98	0.777	0.424	0.273	0.327
	2006	352	337.75	0.984	0.980	0.262	0.816
	2007	355	293.73	0.987	0.910	-0.246	0.739
	2008	300	292.44	0.980	0.987	0.219	0.776
	2009	273	431.09	0.972	1.257	0.632	1.071
2	1962	92	42.66	0.962	0.681	0.004	0.530
	1963	365	536.94	0.967	1.213	-0.243	0.967
	1964	366	173.96	0.986	0.689	-0.024	0.510
	1965	365	386.82	0.972	1.029	-0.014	0.822
	1966	364	277.48	0.979	0.873	0.245	0.680
	1967	347	345.85	0.975	0.998	0.245	0.831
	1968	362	422.58	0.967	1.080	-0.037	0.827
	1969	364	418.73	0.973	1.073	0.550	0.822
	1970	365	489.47	0.965	1.158	0.038	0.934
	1971	347	439.64	0.971	1.126	0.754	0.957
	1972	366	571.42	0.967	1.250	-0.367	0.994
	1973	365	488.82	0.964	1.157	-0.398	0.963
	1974	363	339.04	0.975	0.966	0.015	0.797
	1975	313	346.70	0.972	1.052	-0.073	0.887
	1976	357	378.62	0.969	1.030	-0.311	0.784
	1977	330	382.91	0.972	1.077	-0.414	0.883
	1978	333	241.50	0.980	0.852	-0.029	0.680
	1979	365	267.17	0.980	0.856	0.043	0.701
	1980	182	156.85	0.963	0.928	-0.328	0.742
	1996	195	148.83	0.955	0.874	-0.468	0.663
	1997	213	236.40	0.924	1.053	-0.497	0.808
	1998	245	630.05	0.900	1.604	-0.845	1.228
	1999	166	252.90	0.891	1.234	-0.427	0.855
	2000	229	317.67	0.915	1.178	-0.725	0.917
	2001	365	333.68	0.978	0.956	-0.095	0.647
	2002	345	347.49	0.975	1.004	0.076	0.864
	2003	280	426.45	0.966	1.234	-0.290	0.960
	2004	232	246.32	0.941	1.030	-0.333	0.807
	2005	215	260.75	0.964	1.101	-0.360	0.865
	2006	365	298.09	0.983	0.904	-0.488	0.734
	2007	365	278.07	0.983	0.873	-0.428	0.684
	2008	366	178.78	0.989	0.699	0.060	0.56
	2009	273	214.27	0.984	0.886	-0.370	0.725
3	2002	62	14.03	0.895	0.476	0.195	0.385
	2003	280	229.41	0.982	0.905	-0.345	0.674
	2004	131	182.75	0.745	1.181	-0.298	0.901
	2005	182	138.45	0.983	0.872	-0.264	0.664
	2006	365	239.59	0.986	0.810	-0.372	0.654
	2007	365	204.74	0.988	0.749	-0.294	0.588
	2008	283	130.75	0.991	0.680	0.174	0.508
	2009	157	107.18	0.917	0.826	0.198	0.690

4	1963	92	65.16	0.962	0.842	-0.485	0.663
	1964	356	422.82	0.968	1.090	0.317	0.805
	1965	241	499.91	0.915	1.440	0.798	1.119
	1966	280	880.83	0.888	1.774	1.180	1.390
	1967	333	539.28	0.961	1.273	0.630	1.022
	1968	366	475.33	0.966	1.140	0.191	0.949
	1969	365	1288.29	0.917	1.879	0.239	1.467
	1970	363	397.00	0.973	1.046	0.579	0.816
	1971	336	776.14	0.940	1.520	0.917	1.193
	1972	312	427.72	0.971	1.171	0.076	0.941
	1973	365	567.48	0.963	1.247	0.222	0.944
	1974	365	974.02	0.927	1.634	0.348	1.196
	1975	341	916.15	0.926	1.639	0.089	1.203
	1976	360	413.31	0.972	1.071	-0.021	0.858
	1977	365	411.65	0.976	1.062	0.345	0.795
	1978	365	372.11	0.973	1.010	0.290	0.797
	1979	151	175.31	0.940	1.077	0.540	0.797
	1998	224	472.45	0.917	1.452	-1.087	1.234
	1999	236	240.67	0.950	1.010	-0.597	0.826
	2000	226	464.48	0.913	1.434	-1.131	1.213
	2001	174	310.07	0.847	1.335	-1.059	1.139
	2002	223	197.00	0.978	0.940	-0.238	0.732
	2003	280	287.91	0.976	1.014	-0.405	0.824
	2004	257	351.45	0.964	1.169	-0.404	0.930
	2005	365	374.99	0.975	1.014	-0.350	0.804
	2006	365	537.86	0.966	1.214	-0.042	0.875
	2007	365	363.80	0.979	0.998	-0.193	0.756
	2008	185	121.25	0.932	0.810	-0.046	0.635
	2009	205	147.50	0.979	0.848	0.040	0.681
5	2002	63	71.09	0.442	1.062	-0.438	0.875
	2003	269	273.09	0.975	1.008	-0.251	0.813
	2004	157	255.08	0.909	1.275	-0.335	1.074
	2005	78	59.49	0.780	0.873	-0.396	0.731
	2006	174	162.98	0.980	0.968	-0.033	0.760
	2007	365	352.67	0.980	0.983	0.153	0.781
	2008	274	464.92	0.923	1.303	0.654	1.018
	2009	273	272.45	0.981	0.999	0.450	0.803
6	1965	74	111.61	0.909	1.228	-0.631	1.015
	1966	280	857.02	0.908	1.750	0.796	1.369
	1967	365	752.62	0.960	1.436	-0.669	1.180
	1968	364	2138.92	0.855	2.424	-2.016	2.098
	1969	348	1089.94	0.916	1.770	-0.129	1.355
	1970	298	838.82	0.913	1.678	-1.021	1.383
	1971	345	604.34	0.952	1.324	-0.446	0.976
	1972	366	1233.77	0.912	1.836	-0.130	1.506
	1973	321	617.82	0.953	1.387	-0.206	1.129
	1974	279	712.77	0.920	1.598	-0.571	1.338
	1975	263	1069.97	0.886	2.017	-0.422	1.509
	1976	305	390.66	0.965	1.132	-0.065	0.882
	1977	281	300.71	0.951	1.034	-0.205	0.839
	1978	365	463.83	0.963	1.127	-0.370	0.927
	1979	314	418.63	0.967	1.155	-0.056	0.900
	1980	364	387.38	0.969	1.032	-0.451	0.853
	1981	353	331.22	0.974	0.969	-0.208	0.745
	2001	173	201.87	0.903	1.080	-0.812	0.906
	2002	195	165.40	0.979	0.921	0.125	0.714

	2003	286	102.68	0.991	0.599	-0.092	0.454
	2004	184	137.60	0.957	0.865	-0.432	0.647
	2005	222	922.46	0.884	2.038	-0.403	1.649
	2006	284	1245.30	0.891	2.094	-0.089	1.554
	2008	266	564.68	0.937	1.457	0.767	1.076
	2009	273	337.69	0.977	1.112	0.411	0.874
7	1997	104	100.39	0.921	0.982	-0.755	0.84
	1998	105	91.64	0.846	0.934	-0.107	0.787
	1999	111	82.61	0.857	0.863	-0.173	0.701
	2002	241	246.99	0.969	1.012	-0.189	0.827
	2003	249	121.26	0.985	0.698	-0.319	0.542
	2004	189	235.03	0.928	1.115	-0.550	0.812
	2005	228	1026.35	0.868	2.122	-0.400	1.745
	2006	347	1364.94	0.890	1.983	-0.137	1.496
	2007	70	109.26	0.779	1.249	-1.099	1.110
	2008	366	864.17	0.932	1.537	0.135	1.217
	2009	273	330.50	0.974	1.100	0.248	0.887
8	2003	99	286.03	0.429	1.700	-1.275	1.434
	2004	141	123.81	0.877	0.937	-0.730	0.790
	2005	187	367.98	0.944	1.403	-1.036	1.199
	2006	299	230.52	0.976	0.878	-0.131	0.699
	2007	53	40.08	0.825	0.870	-0.815	0.815
	2008	366	288.71	0.974	0.888	0.261	0.692
	2009	214	437.77	0.945	1.430	0.650	1.165
9	1965	57	291.54	0.181	2.262	-1.965	1.982
	1966	242	1341.91	0.654	2.355	-1.055	1.886
	1967	365	755.29	0.939	1.439	-0.008	1.122
	1968	366	2559.02	0.806	2.644	-1.935	2.219
	1969	253	579.52	0.841	1.513	-0.601	1.212
	1970	75	60.39	0.384	0.897	0.513	0.745
	1971	229	343.43	0.949	1.225	-0.389	1.023
	1972	271	419.84	0.924	1.245	-0.467	1.015
	1973	144	434.25	0.879	1.737	0.985	1.402
	1974	319	323.99	0.964	1.008	-0.558	0.855
	1975	239	395.27	0.955	1.286	-0.337	1.010
	1976	332	761.24	0.923	1.514	-0.502	1.173
	1977	276	835.54	0.918	1.740	-0.937	1.431
	1978	327	701.36	0.924	1.465	-0.794	1.207
	1979	363	540.38	0.961	1.220	-0.655	1.025
	1980	351	533.99	0.943	1.233	-0.775	1.005
	1981	272	743.31	0.917	1.653	-1.058	1.392
	2002	133	202.6	0.806	1.234	0.620	1.008
	2003	179	299.19	0.944	1.293	-0.798	1.078
	2004	366	495.92	0.953	1.164	-0.575	0.948
	2005	364	495.33	0.953	1.167	-0.499	0.976
	2006	362	322.74	0.971	0.944	-0.115	0.825
	2007	359	469.73	0.963	1.144	0.170	0.957
	2008	366	456.04	0.957	1.116	0.301	0.879
	2009	273	518.72	0.950	1.378	0.618	1.108

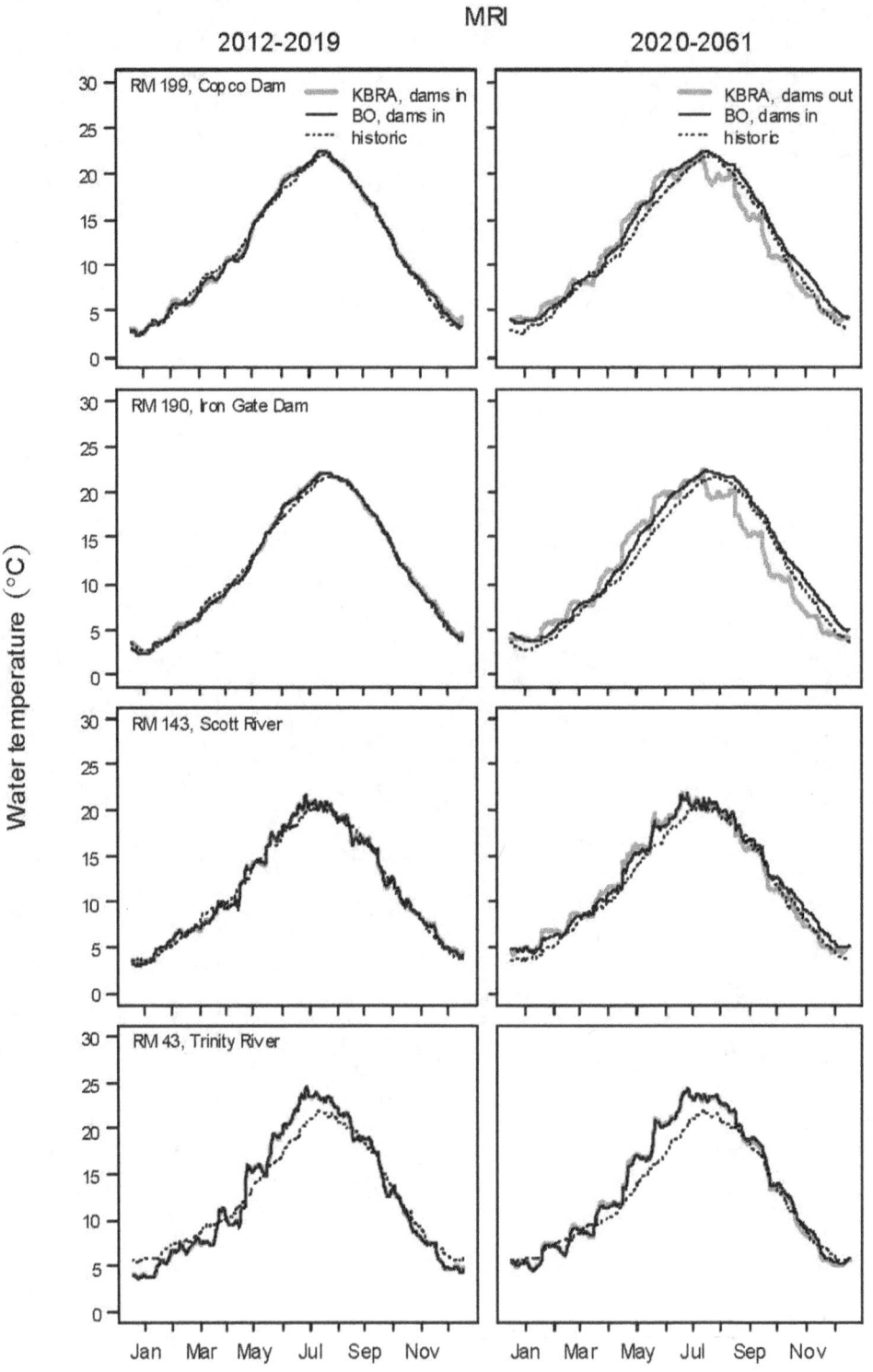

Figure A10. Mean temperature by Julian day for the KBRA dams in period (left panels) and dams out period (right panels) at four locations on the Klamath River for the MRI General Circulation Model (GCM). The historical simulation is shown as a baseline and represents mean temperatures by Julian day for 1961-2009.

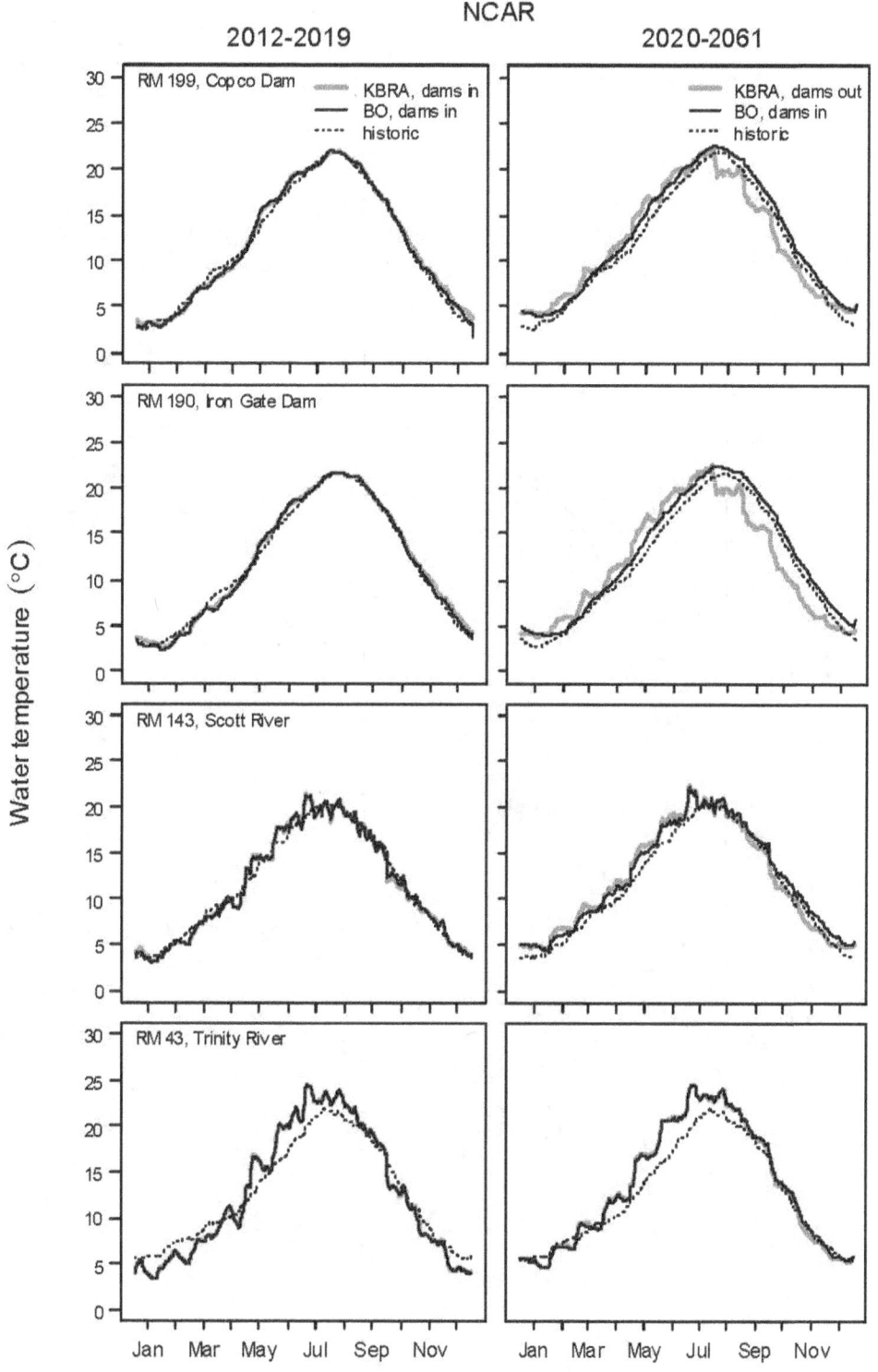

Figure A11. Mean temperature by Julian day for the KBRA dams in period (left panels) and dams out period (right panels) at four locations on the Klamath River for the NCAR General Circulation Model (GCM). The historical simulation is shown as a baseline and represents mean temperatures by Julian day for 1961-2009.

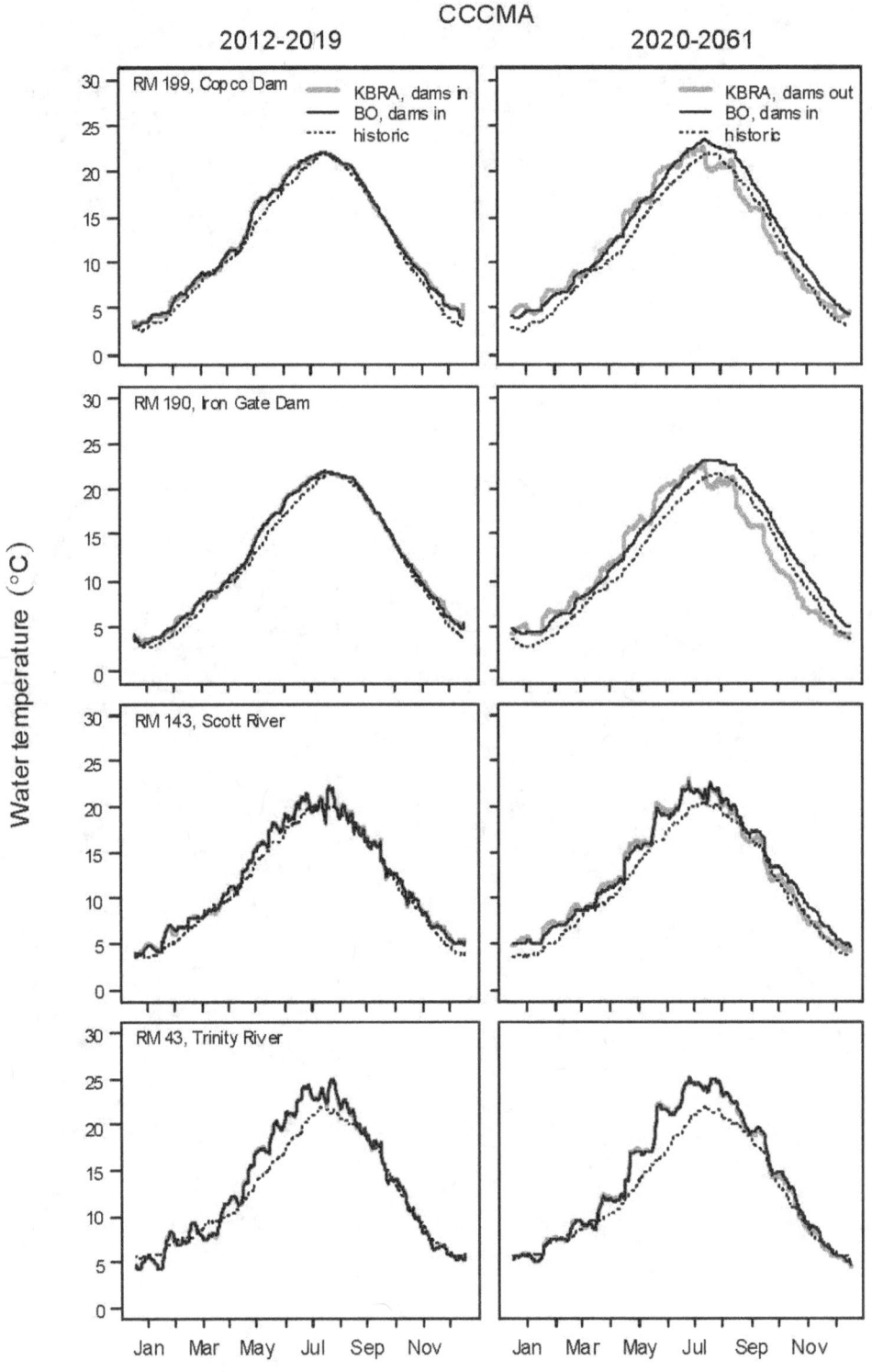

Figure A12. Mean temperature by Julian day for the KBRA dams in period (left panels) and dams out period (right panels) at four locations on the Klamath River for the CCCMA General Circulation Model (GCM). The historical simulation is shown as a baseline and represents mean temperatures by Julian day for 1961–2009.

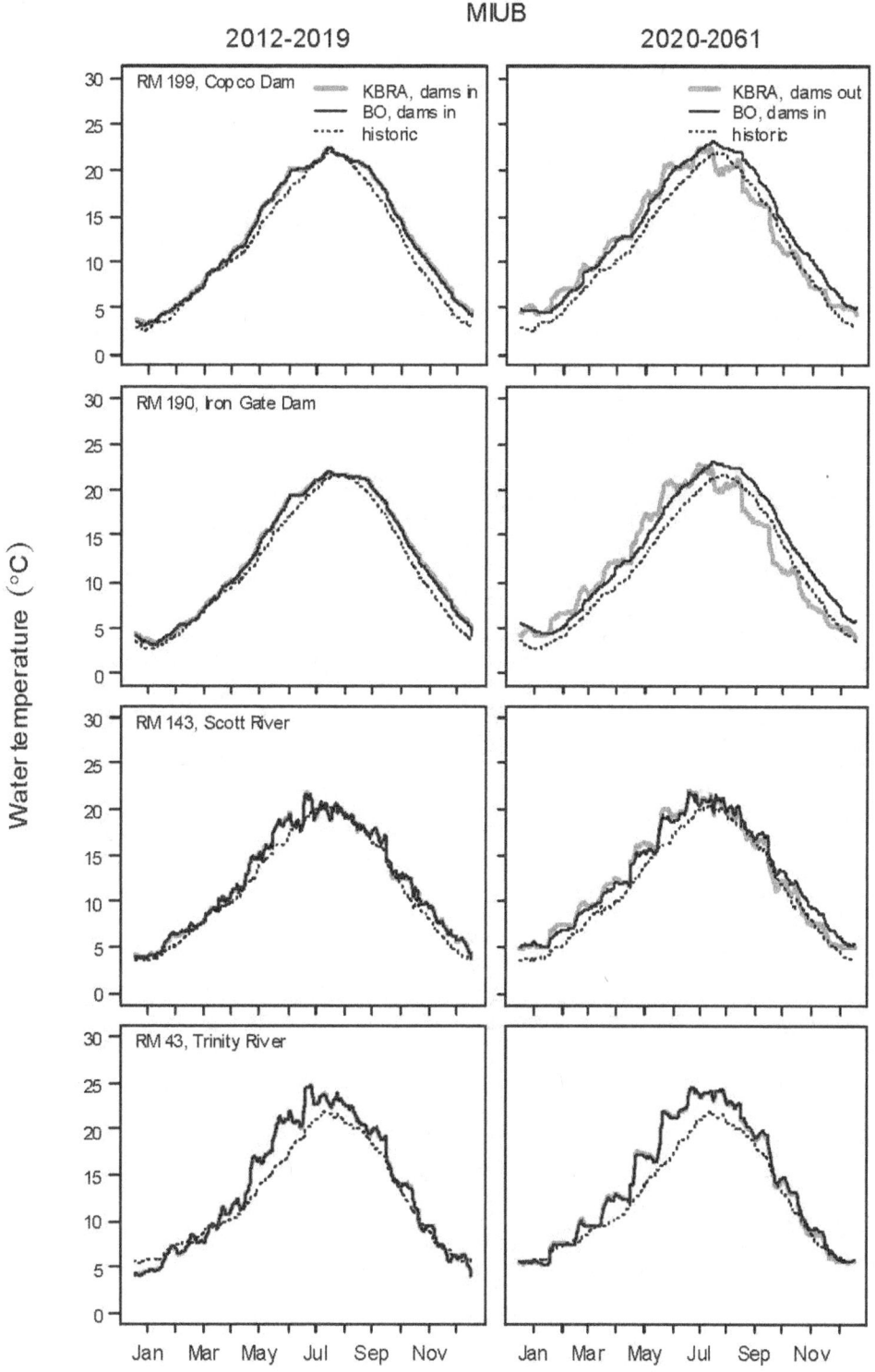

Figure A13. Mean temperature by Julian day for the KBRA dams in period (left panels) and dams out period (right panels) at four locations on the Klamath River for the MIUB General Circulation Model (GCM). The historical simulation is shown as a baseline and represents mean temperatures by Julian day for 1961–2009.